MATHS SKILLS

for

SCIENCE

YEARS 3&4
Scottish Primary 4—5

CREDITS

Author
Louise Petherham

Editor
David Sandford

Assistant Editor
Roanne Davis

Series Designer
Lynne Joesbury

Designer
Rachel Warner

Cover photography
© Stockbyte

Illustrations
Theresa Tibbetts

Published by Scholastic Ltd,
Villiers House,
Clarendon Avenue,
Leamington Spa,
Warwickshire CV32 5PR

Printed by Alden Group Ltd, Oxford

© Scholastic Ltd 2003
Text © Louise Petheram 2003

1 2 3 4 5 6 7 8 9 0   3 4 5 6 7 8 9 0 1 2

British Library Cataloguing-in-Publication Data
A catalogue record for this book is available from the British Library.

ISBN 0-439-98309-6

Acknowledgements

The National Curriculum for England 2000 © Crown Copyright. Reproduced under the terms of HMSO Guidance Note 8. ***The National Numeracy Strategy Framework for Teaching Mathematics*** © Crown Copyright. Reproduced under the terms of HMSO Guidance Note 8. ***A Scheme of Work for Key Stages 1 and 2: Science*** © Qualifications and Curriculum Authority. Reproduced under the terms of HMSO Guidance Note 8. **Scottish 5–14 Guidelines for Environmental Studies** © Crown copyright. Material is reproduced with the permission of the Controller of HMSO and the Queen's Printer for Scotland.

WHY SCIENCE NEEDS MATHS

Maths Skills for Science: Years 3&4/Primary 4–5 aims to assist teachers of children aged 7–9, and is one in a series of three books covering the whole primary age range. This book, and the others in the series, have been designed to develop links between the maths taught in the National Numeracy Strategy and the science topics taught in the QCA Schemes of Work, the National Curriculum for Wales, the National Curriculum for Northern Ireland and the Scottish National Guidelines on Environmental Studies 5–14. The books are thus equally valuable to teachers working in all parts of the UK.

"Almost every scientific investigation or experiment is likely to require one or more of the mathematical skills of classifying, counting, measuring, calculating, estimating, and recording in tables and graphs. In science pupils will, for example, order numbers, including decimals, calculate simple means and percentages, use negative numbers when taking temperatures, decide whether it is more appropriate to use a line graph or bar chart, and plot, interpret and predict from graphs."

Introduction to the NNS *Framework for Teaching Maths*, p17 (March 1999)

The books recognise that for children to be effective learners, they need to develop numeracy skills and science skills in parallel. The present guidelines do not always make the links between science and maths particularly clear, and teachers often find that children need to use particular maths skills within their science lessons that they have not yet learned in their numeracy work. This forces the teacher to use science time for teaching maths skills, leading to a reduction in the 'science value' of the lessons.

Many teachers overcome this problem by co-ordinating their teaching of maths and science to ensure that the relevant maths skills are taught before they are needed in science, or that science topics are taught to reinforce skills learned in maths lessons. But the planning for this can be complicated and time-consuming. The *Maths Skills for Science* books offer a series of co-ordinated maths and science activities that do the planning for you. In addition, the skill levels of the activities are planned to ensure that:

■ the science topics do not require any maths more advanced than that covered in the National Numeracy Strategy for the appropriate year

■ the relevant maths skills are used and reinforced in the science topics.

Developing the maths skills

Progression is built in throughout the series so that the children progress naturally through the skills they need to learn, consolidating and practising at each stage.

Measuring

Activities in the 'Measures' section encourage the children to think about what they need to measure, what apparatus they will need to take the measurement, and whether or not the value they record will be accurate. These skills are developed throughout the three books, and children in Years 3 and 4/Primary 4 and 5 practise selecting suitable measuring apparatus and standard units appropriate to a range of different measuring tasks, and reading more complex measuring scales with an increasing degree of accuracy. Children begin to make decisions about what values they need to measure to ensure results are valid and a fair comparison is made.

Handling data

Although children may successfully collect results from their science activities, they often find it hard to decide on ways to present their findings clearly and appropriately. National tests in science have shown that many children's interpretation skills lag behind skills in other areas, and it is also common for children to have difficulty deciding what conclusions they can infer from their work. For this reason, *Maths Skills for Science* concentrates on the whole process of making results meaningful, recognising that this uses both maths and science skills.

The single 'Handling data' strand of the National Numeracy Strategy has been divided into two sections: 'Recording and organising data' and 'Handling and interpreting data', since these are distinct and specific skills that all scientists need to acquire.

The first of these, 'Recording and organising data', focuses on teaching children to think about why they are presenting results, to identify the important features they wish to show, and to select the best way of organising results to make these aspects clear to a reader. In Years 3 and 4/Primary 4 and 5 the children encounter a wide range of different ways to present data they have collected, such as Carroll diagrams and Venn diagrams, sorting according to one, then two, criteria, and pictograms where one symbol represents more than one item.

In 'Handling and interpreting data', children are challenged to ask themselves: 'What do these results really mean?' and 'What do they tell us?' Children in Years 3 and 4/Primary 4 and 5 interpret frequency tables and bar charts, using these to make comparisons between data and draw simple conclusions.

ABOUT THIS BOOK

The grids on pages 8–9 show how the units in this book link both to the maths skills areas of the National Numeracy Strategy and to the science topics for Year 3 or Year 4/Primary 4–5. The main learning objectives for both maths and science for each unit are given on the grid.

The units in the book cover the full range of science topics, with at least one unit for each topic in each year. Where there are two units for any science topic, these will reinforce or practise different maths skills.

The activities in each book are divided into sections, based on the skill areas from the National Numeracy Strategy. In this book, the skill areas covered are:

- Solving problems
- Measures
- Shape and space
- Recording and organising data
- Handling and interpreting data.

This book assumes that the majority of children will have mastered the basic skills of understanding numbers and the number system that they will need for their science, and the emphasis is on increasing understanding of the processes of measuring, recording and presenting data, and on interpreting data in a variety of forms.

The activities for each year group assume that the children will achieve approximately Level 2 or 3, Scottish Level B, at the end of Year 3/Primary 4 and Level 3, Scottish Level B/C, by the end of Year 4/Primary 5. Extension activities are provided for the more able children and support activities for the less able.

INTRODUCTION

The activities in this book are made up of six-page units. Each unit focuses specifically on a science topic from one of the two years covered, and uses maths skills developed within the National Numeracy Strategy for that year. Each unit is made up of two pages of teacher's notes and four supporting photocopiable pages, as detailed below.

A maths lesson planning page containing:

■ learning objectives derived from the National Numeracy Strategy

■ a suggested introduction and whole-class teacher-directed activity

■ a follow-up children's activity consisting of individual or group work

■ ideas for differentiation for more able and less able children

■ a 'Science link' activity that provides maths resources to reinforce the skill taught in the maths lesson within a science context:

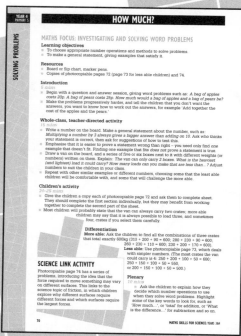

A science lesson planning page containing:

■ learning objectives derived from the QCA Schemes of Work, or the corresponding documents for Scotland, Northern Ireland or Wales

■ a suggested introduction and whole-class, teacher-directed activity

■ a follow-up children's activity consisting of individual or group work

■ ideas for differentiation for more able and less able children

■ suggested links to other subject areas within the National Curriculum.

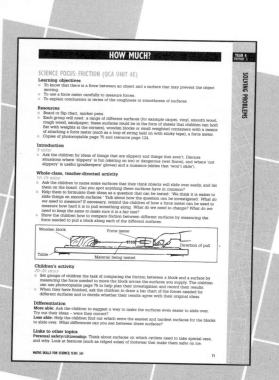

Four photocopiable pages:

- a worksheet supporting the maths activity
- a worksheet supporting the 'Science link' activity
- a worksheet supporting the science activity
- a supplementary page, which may provide a supporting maths activity for less able children, or a resource or recording sheet for one of the maths or science activities.

Throughout the book approximate timings are given for the activities in both maths and science lessons. The lessons are intended to last a maximum of 60 minutes, but there is flexibility to lengthen or shorten particular sections to suit your specific needs. In some cases the lesson may need to be divided as children will be collecting results for an activity over several days.

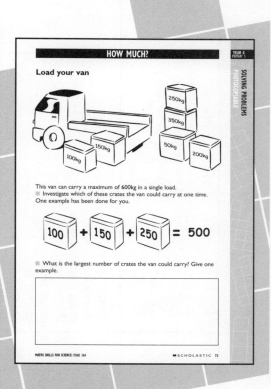

Also included at the back of the book are photocopiable resource pages that can be used with several of the units. Sometimes these are listed with the resources required for individual units but you might also find them useful in other units – or other activities altogether. These include a sheet for drawing bar charts, a sheet for drawing pictograms where children determine how many items one pictogram symbol represents, sheets for drawing two different types of Venn diagrams and two different types of Carroll diagrams, and a final 'Pupil record sheet'. This last page allows the children to make a note of each activity as they complete it, and the learning they have gained from it. This record will, in addition, allow you to follow each child's developing maths skills as he or she progresses through Years 3 and 4/Primary 4 and 5, and help you to identify children who might need particular types of support with forthcoming activities.

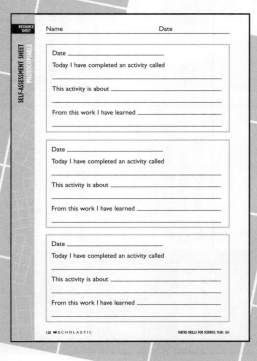

YEAR 3 MATHS AND SCIENCE LINKS

MATHS STRANDS \ SCIENCE TOPICS	TEETH AND EATING	HELPING PLANTS GROW WELL	CHARACTERISTICS OF MATERIALS	ROCKS AND SOILS	MAGNETS AND SPRINGS	LIGHT AND SHADOWS
SOLVING PROBLEMS					**Finding patterns** Recognising patterns. Predicting the effect of stretching elastic bands different amounts.	
MEASURES		**Choosing amounts** Suggesting suitable units and measuring apparatus. Making careful observations and measurements of plants growing.	**How stretchy?** Measuring length using standard units. Making a fair comparison of the stretchiness of different tights.	**Comparing volumes** Measuring volume using standard units. Making accurate measurements of time and volume.		
SHAPE AND SPACE				**Classifying with Venn diagrams** Classifying objects according to one or two criteria. Grouping rocks according to observable characteristics.		**Sundials** Understanding angles as a measure of turn. Knowing that shadows change length and position during the day.
RECORDING AND ORGANISING DATA	**Food survey** Using Caroll diagrams. Knowing that animals, including humans, need food to grow and be active.					
HANDLING AND INTERPRETING DATA	**Food preferences** Presenting and interpreting data. Investigating the food eaten by different animals.	**What do bar charts show?** Making bar charts. Recognising that plant growth is affected by temperature.	**Choose the best** Using frequency tables. Comparing different cloths and drawing conclusions.			

YEAR 4 MATHS AND SCIENCE LINKS

MATHS STRANDS \ SCIENCE TOPICS	MOVING AND GROWING	HABITATS	KEEPING WARM	SOLIDS, LIQUIDS AND HOW THEY CAN BE SEPARATED	FRICTION	CIRCUITS AND CONDUCTORS
SOLVING PROBLEMS					**How much?** Investigating and solving word problems. Knowing that there is a friction force between a moving object and a surface.	**Shining brightly** Using language related to measures. Suggesting ways to change the brightness of bulbs in a circuit.
MEASURES			**Making accurate measurements** Reading measuring scales. Making careful measurements of temperature and time.			
SHAPE AND SPACE	**Turning and bending** Recognising angles. Knowing that humans are supported by a bony skeleton.					
RECORDING AND ORGANISING DATA		**Wildlife investigations** Collecting data to solve a problem. Asking questions and making predictions to solve problems.		**Sorting and separating** Sorting with Venn diagrams. Knowing that solids can be mixed and it is often possible to get original materials back.		
HANDLING AND INTERPRETING DATA	**Comparing boys and girls** Using bar charts to make comparisons. Knowing that human skeletons grow as humans grow.		**How many, how much?** Drawing and interpreting bar charts. Using ICT to collect and display temperatures.		**Understanding bar charts** Interpreting bar charts. Planning a fair test, deciding what to change and what to keep the same.	

SOLVING PROBLEMS

FINDING PATTERNS

MATHS FOCUS: RECOGNISING PATTERNS

Learning objectives
■ To recognise simple patterns and relationships.
■ To make generalisations and predictions.

Resources
■ Coloured cubes.
■ Squared paper, coloured pencils, number lines.
■ Copies of photocopiable pages 12 (page 13 for less able children) and 14.

Introduction
5 mins

■ Ask the children: *What is a pattern?* Talk about some patterns in real life, such as wallpaper with repeating pictures, or a repeating rule in a game like dominoes, where you always add a tile with the same picture or number as the last one in the row.

Whole-class, teacher-directed activity
15 mins

■ Tell the children: *Sometimes we make patterns with numbers.* Start to count on from 1 in ones. *What am I doing?* (Adding on 1 each time.)
■ Count on in twos, starting from 2. *Now what am I doing?* Count on in ones and twos from different numbers; ask the children to join in as soon as they recognise the pattern.
■ Try counting using more complex patterns, for example counting back in ones and twos, or counting on in larger numbers each time. Again, ask children to join in as soon as they can. Can they describe what the pattern is?
■ Make simple patterns with cubes, such as *red cube, blue cube, red cube, blue cube.* Ask individual children to continue the pattern, then ask others to suggest and make their own patterns with the cubes. *Who can tell me what the pattern of these cubes is?*

Children's activity
25–30 mins

■ Give each child a copy of photocopiable page 12. Ask them first to identify each of the patterns shown, then to continue the pattern. Provide each group with cubes and number lines so that children can copy the pattern with real objects if they need to.

■ Ask the children to make up some patterns of their own with both numbers and cubes, recording their patterns on squared paper as numbers or coloured squares.

Differentiation
More able: Ask pairs of children to invent more complicated patterns to try out on each other. Encourage them to try making patterns that include both adding and multiplying, such as *add on 1, double it, add on 1, double it.* Can each work out the rule for a pattern the other has invented?

Less able: Use photocopiable page 13, which shows less complicated patterns. Encourage less confident children to work in pairs, using cubes to make simple patterns suggested by each other.

SCIENCE LINK ACTIVITY

Photocopiable page 14 provides an opportunity for children to spot patterns in 'real' situations. The table shows how far an arrow flies as the string of a bow is stretched more. Children should be able to use this data to identify a pattern in the distance the arrow flies as the stretch of the bow increases, and then use this to make a prediction about other terms in the pattern.

Plenary
10 mins

Look at some of the children's patterns. Ask other children to suggest what would come next, and to describe the rule used to make the pattern. Are they right?

MATHS SKILLS FOR SCIENCE: YEARS 3&4

SCIENCE FOCUS: MAGNETS AND SPRINGS (QCA UNIT 3E)

Learning objectives
■ To make predictions of the effect of stretching elastic bands by different amounts.
■ To make comparisons and identify patterns in results.

Resources
■ Strong elastic bands (those used around bundles of post are ideal) of varying length and thickness, sheets of paper.

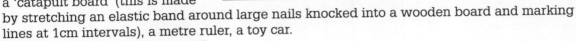

elastic band stretched between large nails — wooden board — lines at 1cm intervals

■ Each group of children will need a 'catapult board' (this is made by stretching an elastic band around large nails knocked into a wooden board and marking lines at 1cm intervals), a metre ruler, a toy car.
■ Copies of photocopiable page 15.

Safety: Make sure that the children are aware of the dangers of over-stretching elastic bands, and of the risk of injury to themselves and others if they are not used sensibly.

Introduction
5 mins
■ Ask: *Who can tell me something about pushes or pulls?* Discuss some familiar pushes and pulls: opening a door or pushing a swing. Introduce *force* as a word meaning a push or a pull.
■ Pass round some elastic bands for the children to practise stretching. Talk about what they can feel: *Can you feel the direction of the force?* (It pulls the band back to its original shape.)

Whole-class, teacher-directed activity
10–15 mins
■ Show the children a selection of different elastic bands. Ask: *How can we find out how big the force from these elastic bands is?* Ask the children to test the 'pull' using their hands. Do different elastic bands feel different when they are stretched?
■ Try putting different elastic bands round sheets of paper. Discuss what happens and why. (A stretched elastic band will crumple the paper because it exerts a force on the paper.)
■ Explain that the force from some elastic bands is bigger than the force from others. Ask: *When might the force be biggest – from the thickest, or the most stretched band?* (There is a general pattern: the thicker the band, the stronger the force.) Children can test this by stretching different thicknesses of band by the same amount and feeling which pulls back hardest. Ask them to predict the effect of stretching a band by different amounts.

Children's activity
20–25 mins
■ Demonstrate how the elastic band on the catapult board can propel a toy car. Ask: *How could we use this board to investigate how the amount of stretch affects how far the car travels?*
■ Working in small groups, children should use the catapult board to see what effect stretching the elastic band has on the distance the car travels. The lines on the catapult board make sure that the 'amount of stretch' increases steadily; the children should measure carefully how far their car goes each time. Results can be recorded on photocopiable page 15.
■ Ask the children to use their table of data to identify a pattern in the results, and to make predictions about how far the car would travel if the elastic band were stretched more.

Differentiation
More able: Ask groups to predict, then test, the effect of using weaker elastic bands on how far the car travels. Some may even be able to suggest other things that would affect how far the car went (roughness of board, weight of car).
Less able: Children may need support in measuring and recording. Ask them to focus on the question: *What happens to the distance the car travels when we stretch the elastic band more?*

Links to other topics
Design and technology: Look at ways of making a toy move (such as a balloon-powered plane).

Spot the pattern

■ Write or draw the next two terms in these patterns.

1.   2   5   8   11 _____   _____

2.

■ Can you spot the patterns here? Write or draw the next two terms in
each pattern.

1.   1   2   4   7   11   16   _____   _____

2.   1   2   4   8   16   _____   _____

3.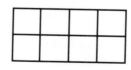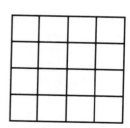

NOW TRY THIS   Make up some more patterns of your own.

FINDING PATTERNS

Making patterns

This is an 'Add on 2' pattern.

■ Use a number line to work out the next two terms.
Write them down.

2   4   6   8   _____   _____

■ Draw the next two terms in these patterns.

■ Draw a pattern that adds on two blocks each time. It has been started for you.

NOW
TRY
THIS
Can you draw this pattern of blocks in a different way?

FINDING PATTERNS

Who's the best archer?

Some children in Class 3 tried a 'Fire an arrow' activity on their History Day.

This table shows how far they each stretched the string and how far the arrow went.

Name	How far bowstring stretched (cm)	How far arrow went (m)
Mr Tops (the teacher)	1	
Ryan	2	3
Amy	3	5
Jyoti	4	7
Clare	5	9
Abdul	6	

How far do you think Mr Tops's arrow would go? What about Abdul's arrow? Write your answers in the table.

Anila wants to fire the arrow furthest. How far will she have to stretch the bowstring?

NOW TRY THIS Write a sentence to explain what happens to the arrow as the bowstring is stretched more.

Elastic band power

■ Use a 'catapult board' to see how far a toy car will move when you use the force of an elastic band to push it.

■ Fill in the table to show how far the car moves.

Distance elastic band is pulled back (cm)	Distance car travels (cm)
1	
2	
3	
4	
5	

■ Complete this sentence:

The further the elastic band is stretched _____

_____

How far do you think the car would go if the elastic band was pulled back 6cm?

I think the car would travel _____ cm.

NOW TRY THIS What would happen if you used a different elastic band?

HOW STRETCHY?

MATHS FOCUS: MEASURING LENGTH USING STANDARD UNITS

Learning objectives
- To measure and compare lengths using standard units.
- To read the value shown by a ruler or tape measure to the nearest half centimetre.
- To suggest suitable units and measuring equipment for measuring length.

Resources
- Metre rulers, tape measures, a range of items of uniform and non-uniform shape to measure (books, cushions, pencil cases, vases, scarves, string and so on).
- Copies of photocopiable pages 18 (page 19 for less able children) and 20.

Introduction
5 mins
- Practise measuring objects where the start and end point of the measurement is clear, such as the width of a book or the circumference of a cylinder. Choose some objects that would be measured most appropriately with a ruler, and some that would be measured with a tape measure. How would the children decide which to use? Practise reading values to the nearest half-centimetre.

Whole-class, teacher-directed activity
10 mins
- Show the children some objects whose distance to measure is not clear, such as the distance around a non-uniform vase, the width of a cushion, or the length of a scarf.
- Ask: *If we want to measure this object, should we use a tape measure or a ruler? Where shall we put the ruler?* Discuss sensible measurements for each object: *We could measure the widest part of the vase, otherwise people might think it was tiny and it isn't; ...along the edge of the cushion because the middle is scrunched up and hard to measure.*
- Let volunteers measure some of the objects. Do other children agree with their choice of place to measure, their choice of measuring apparatus and the measurement they get?

Children's activity
20–25 mins
- Children should work in pairs to measure a range of different objects with non-uniform shapes. Encourage them to decide together what measurement they should take and what apparatus to use. Photocopiable page 18 can be used to record, in drawing and writing, the objects measured, their choices and their results.

Differentiation
More able: Ask more confident children to decide whether one measurement is sufficient (for example: *You really need to say how tall the vase is as well as how wide, otherwise people won't know what it is like*).

Less able: Give children photocopiable page 19 to make notes on, as this provides more guidance on what measurements to take.

SCIENCE LINK ACTIVITY

In small groups, ask children to measure and compare the sizes of their school jumpers. Photocopiable page 20 can be used to record any decisions the group makes about what measurements to take, how to make the comparison fair (lay all jumpers flat, measure across the same part and so on) and the results they get.

Plenary
10 mins
- Use children's work to show that there are lots of different measurements that can be taken for an object, and that they are all useful as long as we know from where the measurement was taken. Discuss why it is important to say or show where the measurement was taken. ('The vase was 10cm' doesn't really tell us much, but 'The vase was 10cm tall' does.)

SCIENCE FOCUS: CHARACTERISTICS OF MATERIALS (QCA UNIT 3C)

Learning objectives
- To plan how to find out which pair of tights is most stretchy, making a fair comparison.
- To decide what to change, what to keep the same and what to measure.
- To make careful measurements of length.

Resources
- Samples of different types and sizes of tights (different denier, 'support' tights, thick cotton tights and so on), enough for at least two pairs per group. Each pair of tights should have a different letter or number pinned to them. Tape measures, string, weights.
- Copies of photocopiable page 21 and resource page 124.

Introduction
5 mins
- Show the children a pair of tights. Ask: *How can we measure how long these are?* Discuss where to measure from and to, and the importance of taking the same measurements for all pairs of tights if they are to be compared with one another.

Whole class, teacher-directed activity
10 mins

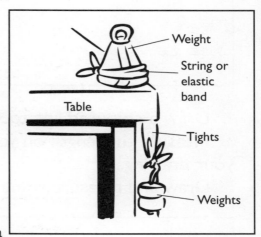

- Ask: *What happens to the tights if I pull them? Do all tights stretch by the same amount? How could we find out?*
- Help the children plan an investigation to compare the stretchiness of different pairs of tights. Discuss what they will need to measure (how long the tights were before and after they were stretched), what to change (the pair of tights), and how they can make a fair comparison (change only one thing at a time, always measure to the same point on the tights).
- Think about how to set up the investigation: how to fasten the tights, what measuring apparatus to use, how to record results and so on. Tights can be held firmly by using a loop of string around the waist, held in place by a heavy object on a table, allowing the tights to dangle over the edge. This has the advantage that weights will be near the floor, doing less damage if they fall.

Children's activity
20–25 mins
- Children should work in small groups to compare the stretchiness of different pairs of tights, using photocopiable page 21 to guide their investigation and record their results. Give each group one pair of tights initially, telling them to change them from a central 'store' when they have completed each set of measurements.
- Once they have collected results for four pairs of tights, children should plot a bar chart of their results, using resource page 124, to compare how much different pairs of tights stretch.
- Look at different groups' results and talk about what the children found to establish which kind of tights were most stretchy.

Differentiation
More able: Encourage the children to consider the effect of the thickness of the tights and their initial size (children's or adults). Do they have enough data to draw any conclusions about the type of tights that are most stretchy?
Less able: Can the children use their bar charts to list the tights they tested in order from 'stretched most' to 'stretched least'?

Links to other topics
Literacy: Ask the children to make up imaginative stories or mini-plays about 'The tights that wouldn't stop stretching'. **History:** What clothes did people wear in other times?

HOW STRETCHY?

Measuring non-uniform objects

What object will you measure? Draw it in the space below.

■ Draw a coloured line to show the length you will measure.
■ Measure the length on your real object. Write the length on your drawing.
■ Draw and measure some more objects.

NOW TRY THIS Is one measurement enough to tell someone what your object is like? Draw and measure some more distances you might investigate.

Measuring non-uniform objects

■ Choose a book to measure. Draw it here.

How wide is it? Write it on your drawing.
How tall is it? Write it on your drawing.

■ Draw a non-uniform object (an 'odd' shape that is hard to measure).

■ Draw a line on your picture to show what length you measure.
■ Measure the length on your real object. Write the measurement on your drawing.

NOW TRY THIS Can you draw and measure other objects?

HOW STRETCHY?

Whose jumper is biggest?

■ Draw your school jumper.

■ Draw a line to show the distance you are going to measure.
■ Measure all the jumpers in your group. Fill in the table.

Whose jumper?	Our measurement (cm)

Whose jumper is biggest? _____

Whose jumper is smallest? _____

NOW TRY THIS How did you make your comparison fair?

HOW STRETCHY?

Which tights stretch most?

■ Draw a diagram to show what you did.

■ Write your results in the table.

Tights	Unstretched length (cm)	Stretched length (cm)	How much they stretched (cm)

■ Draw a bar chart to show how much different pairs of tights stretched.

In your group, which pair of tights stretched most? _____

In the class, which tights stretched most? _____

NOW TRY THIS Can you draw a conclusion?

COMPARING VOLUMES

MATHS FOCUS: MEASURING VOLUME

Learning objectives
- To measure and compare volumes using standard units.
- To read a measuring scale to the nearest marked division.

Resources
- Water; food colouring; a range of containers of different shapes and volumes (each group will need five containers labelled with different letters or numbers), and some identical ones; a range of measuring cylinders.
- Four containers per group – two identical small containers and two identical large containers (the large containers should hold approximately twice the volume of the small ones; one of each size of container should have identical holes in the base so that the small container empties in about 3 minutes), a large bowl or tray to catch the water, simple timers.
- Copies of photocopiable pages 24 and 25.

Introduction
5 mins
- Show the children a container of water (adding food colouring makes the water show up better). Ask: *How can we find out how much water is in this container?* Discuss standard and uniform non-standard methods for measuring volume.

Whole-class, teacher-directed activity
15 mins
- Show the children two identical containers, each with a different amount of water in. Ask: *How can we tell which has more water in it?* (The containers are identical, so we can use direct comparison.)
- Repeat with different-shaped, but similar-sized containers. Ask for volunteers to use measuring cylinders to decide which container has more water in it. Ask other children to choose other appropriately sized measuring beakers to check that the readings are correct.

Children's activity
25–30 mins
- Provide small groups of children with five different-sized containers. Ask them to use measurement to find out how much each container holds, placing the containers in order of their capacity and recording their findings on photocopiable page 24. Give children a choice of different measuring beakers and encourage them to choose the most suitable size to measure each volume.

SCIENCE LINK ACTIVITY

This activity allows children to practise making predictions and timing how long water takes to flow from different containers. Ask small groups to measure and record the volumes of two different-sized containers, then to measure the time taken for water to flow out from the smaller container (when filled to the top). From this information, encourage the children to use their knowledge about the size of the containers to predict how long it will take for the water to flow out from the larger container. Photocopiable page 25 contains instructions and space to record results.

Differentiation
More able: Ask the children questions such as: *Find the container that holds closest to 200ml*, or *How many times could you fill the smallest container from the largest container?*
Less able: Help the children with recording their results. They may need reminding to catch any water they spill so that they get an accurate measurement.

Plenary
10 mins
Talk with the children about how they decided which was the most suitable measuring beaker to use in each case, and how they decided which division to read the scale to when the water was not 'on the line'.

SCIENCE FOCUS: ROCKS AND SOILS (QCA UNIT 3D)

Learning objectives
■ To make and record measurements of time and volume of water.
■ To use results to make comparisons, draw and explain conclusions.
■ To know that there are different types of soil.

Resources
Board or flip chart, marker pens, two potted plants (one with very dry soil, one with very wet soil), water, containers to catch water.
■ Each group will need three identical small containers with holes in the base (yoghurt pots are ideal), samples of three different types of soil (such as sand, clay, and leaf mould or potting compost), sticky labels, a measuring beaker, a stopwatch or simple timer.
■ Copies of photocopiable pages 26 and 27.
Safety: If using soil samples in the classroom, collect them from areas uncontaminated by dog faeces or broken glass. You may prefer to make up your own soil samples.

Introduction
5 mins
■ Ask: *Who can tell me something about soils?* Recap the children's knowledge about soils, making a list on the board of what they know already. Make sure the children are aware that there are different types of soil, and that soil is made up from particles, which can be different sizes. Children may also be able to describe differences in colour and texture for different soils, and state that puddles stay longer on some soils than others.

Whole-class, teacher-directed activity
10–15 mins
■ Show the children the two potted plants. Ask them to describe the soil in each pot. Hold up the pots and ask children to suggest what might happen when you pour water on the soil in each pot.
■ Pour a small amount of water on the dry pot and a large amount of water on the wet pot, so it overflows or runs through. Ask: *Does water flow more easily through some soils than others?* Then ask: *When I watered the plants just now, was it a fair test?* (It wasn't because one soil was wet and one dry to begin with, and you used different amounts of water.)
■ Show the children the yoghurt pots and soil samples. Discuss how you might carry out a fair test to compare how water flows through different soils. Emphasise the need for fair testing – the children will need to pour equal volumes of water on dry samples of all the soils, one at a time, and record either how long it takes before the soil stops dripping or how much water flows through.

Children's activity
20–25 mins
■ Working in small groups, children should investigate the flow of water through different soil samples, using one of the methods described in the whole-class activity. Encourage children to think about making careful measurements and making fair comparisons as they go. Soils should be tested one at a time, not simultaneously, as this makes results easier to record. Photocopiable pages 26 and 27 guide children through each activity and give space for recording results. Help children to explain their results: 'The clay particles are very small and packed together tightly. There isn't much room left for the water to get through.'

Differentiation
More able: Ask the children to predict which type of soil they tested will dry most quickly after rain. Which would be best for a playing field? Why?
Less able: Children may benefit from modelling the flow of water through soils by dropping salt (water) through containers of large and small beads (different-sized soil particles).

Links to other topics
Environment/habitat: Look at how different soils affect the plants and animals that grow and live there.

COMPARING VOLUMES

How much water does it hold?

▧ Place your containers side by side.
Which one do you think holds the most? Draw them in order.

Holds least				Holds most

▧ Now measure how much each container holds.

▧ Write the volume of each container underneath your pictures.

Was your prediction correct? _____

How much does the biggest container hold? _____

How much does the smallest container hold? _____

How many containers hold more than 100ml? _____

How many times could the biggest container fill up the smallest?

_____

Which container holds closest to 200ml? _____

COMPARING VOLUMES

How quickly does it empty?

You should have four containers.

■ Find the volume of the two containers without holes.

Volume of small container = _____ ml.

Volume of large container = _____ ml.

■ Now use the small container with holes in.
■ Fill it with water.

■ Lift it up and start your timer.

■ Measure how long it takes for the container to empty. Write it down.

Time taken for the small container to empty = _____ s.

How long do you think it will take the large container to empty?

I predict the large container will take _____ to empty.

■ Now measure it.

Time taken for the large container to empty = _____ s.

Was your prediction correct? _____

COMPARING VOLUMES

How quickly does water flow through soils?

■ Fill each container with a different type of soil.

■ Put the same amount of soil in each container. Pack it down well.

■ Label each type of soil.

■ Hold the first soil sample over the bowl.

■ Start the timer.

■ **Slowly** pour on 100ml of water.

■ Stop the timer when the soil stops dripping.

■ Record the time in the table.

Type of soil	Time to stop dripping (s)

NOW TRY THIS Which soil does water flow through most quickly?

COMPARING VOLUMES

How much water flows through soils?

■ Fill each container with a different type of soil.

■ Put the same amount of soil in each container. Pack it down well.

■ Label each type of soil.

■ Draw diagrams to show how to find out how much water drips through each type of soil.

■ Pour 100ml of water onto each type of soil.

■ Use the table to record the volume of water that drips through each type of soil.

Type of soil	Volume of water collected (cm³)

NOW TRY THIS   Which soil would be best for a playing field? Why?

CHOOSING AMOUNTS

MATHS FOCUS: CHOOSING APPROPRIATE MEASURING APPARATUS

Learning objectives
- To suggest suitable units to measure length and capacity.
- To suggest and use simple measuring equipment, reading number scales accurately.

Resources
- Apparatus for measuring length (rulers and tape measures) and capacity (spoons and jugs).
- A selection of objects of different lengths and containers of different capacities.
- Copies of photocopiable pages 30 (page 31 for less able children) and 32.

Introduction
5–10 mins
- Ask: *What would you use to measure the length of something?* Make sure that the children are familiar with standard units (centimetres and metres).
- Show the children some apparatus for measuring length (a 30cm ruler, metre stick, tape measures). Ask: *What might we measure with these?* Discuss their suggestions.
- Repeat the above for capacity, making sure the children understand what capacity is and know some of the units used.

Whole-class, teacher-directed activity
10–15 mins
- Talk about how to select appropriate apparatus – would you use a metre ruler to measure the length of an eraser? Is it more accurate to measure a curved edge with a tape measure?
- Show the children an object and ask: *What should we use to measure the length of this?* Ask a volunteer to choose a suitable piece of apparatus and measure the object's length. Ask others to decide whether they have chosen the most appropriate apparatus, explaining why.
- Repeat the activity, this time choosing suitable equipment to measure the capacity of an object. Again, encourage the children to make, and explain, sensible choices.

Children's activity
25–30 mins
- Working in groups, ask the children to measure the length or capacity of a range of different objects. They should use photocopiable page 30 to write down their choice of measuring apparatus and record their measurements. Explain that careful measuring is important, but the emphasis of this lesson should be on making appropriate choices of measuring apparatus.

Differentiation
More able: Ask children to compare similar lengths or capacities, suggesting which apparatus might be most accurate and why.

Less able: Provide objects where the choice of measuring apparatus is easy (lengths close to 1m, and so on). Use photocopiable page 31 to help children choose measuring apparatus. They can solve the second problem in two ways – number of spoonfuls in the bottle, or by pouring the contents into a larger jug. Either method is acceptable.

SCIENCE LINK ACTIVITY

Photocopiable page 32 allows the children to practise choosing appropriate measuring apparatus in the context of the amount of water different-sized house plants might need. They should record their choices in labelled drawings on the worksheet. When estimating the amount of water the second house plant would need, expect simple, but reasoned, answers – 'It's about twice as high as a normal houseplant so I think it will need twice as much water.'

Plenary
10 mins
Ask some children to explain their choice of measuring apparatus for particular tasks. Ask children to suggest other objects they could measure with each of the pieces of measuring apparatus they used.

SCIENCE FOCUS: HELPING PLANTS GROW WELL (QCA UNIT 3B)

Learning objectives
■ To make careful observations and measurements of plants as they grow.
■ To know that plants need water, but not unlimited water, for healthy growth.

Resources
■ Two seedlings: one well-watered and healthy, and one that has died from lack of water.
■ Each group will need one well-watered healthy seedling (fast-growing seedlings, such as beans, are ideal), sticky labels, pens, a range of apparatus for measuring height and capacity.
■ A copy of photocopiable page 33 for each child, A4 paper.

Introduction
5 mins
■ Ask the children how many of them have house plants at home, or know someone who does. Talk about how the plants are looked after, where they are kept, what they are grown in, whether or not they are given water or plant food and if so, how often.

Whole-class, teacher-directed activity
10–15 mins
■ Show the children one healthy seedling and one dead seedling. Ask them to describe the differences between the two (size, shape, colour of leaves and so on). Allow children to feel the soil in each pot, and ask them to suggest why one of the seedlings died.
■ Talk about other circumstances where the children have seen the effect of plants not having any water (such as house plants dying if you forget to water them, lawns going brown in hot summer weather, garden plants wilting if it doesn't rain for a long time).
■ Ask: *How much water do plants need? Does it matter how much water they get?* Discuss how the seedlings you have could be used to find out if it matters how much water plants are given.

Children's activity
20–25 mins
■ Plan this investigation together as a class first. You will need to return to it every week or so over a month or more to see how the children's seedlings grow.
■ Talk about how to plan a fair test (change only the amount of water, keeping everything else the same for all the seedlings). Decide how much water each group should give their seedling and how often. Make sure the children understand they must give their seedling the agreed amount of water, even if it begins to die – children sometimes worry that the investigation isn't working properly if their seedlings die.
■ Talk about what the children are going to measure, and how to decide which is the healthiest seedling. Remind the children of the two plants they looked at earlier.
■ Each group should choose appropriate apparatus to measure the volume of water to give and to measure the height of their seedling. Give each group a copy of photocopiable page 33 to plan their investigation, and a sheet of paper to record their results on in words and pictures.
■ Complete the last section of the worksheet after a plenary session, sharing the results from all the groups. Children should find that too much or too little water both stop the seedlings growing well.

Differentiation
This activity should be accessible to all children, working in mixed-ability groups.
More able: Ask the children to explain their choice of measuring position. For example: 'we measured to the top of the stem because the leaves might wilt if it's a hot day.'
Less able: Children should concentrate on selecting suitable measuring apparatus, not deciding the best point to measure seedling height to – provide help with this if necessary.

Links to other topics
Geography: Investigate why food plants do not always grow well in hot, dry countries, contributing to famine. **Craft/technology:** Design and make small plant containers, using clay (varnish them well on the inside before use).

CHOOSING AMOUNTS

What shall we use to measure it?

■ Look at this measuring apparatus.

■ **Circle** those used to measure capacity.
■ **Tick** those used to measure length.

■ Fill in this table. The first one has been done for you.

What we measured	What equipment we used	How big it was
		19cm

NOW TRY THIS Suggest some things you might measure in kilometres or thousands of litres.

CHOOSING AMOUNTS

How much does it hold?

What volume of water might this bath hold? Circle the apparatus you would use to find out.

What volume of medicine does this bottle hold? Circle two pieces of apparatus that you could use to find out.

■ Draw something you could measure with each of these.

CHOOSING AMOUNTS

How much water do they need?

■ Draw and label suitable apparatus to measure the amount of water these plants need each day.

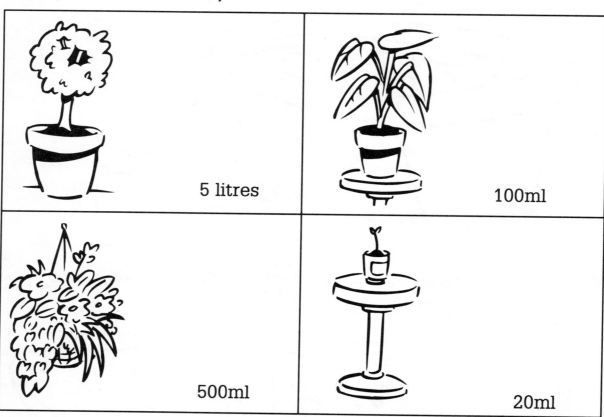

5 litres

100ml

500ml

20ml

■ Draw the apparatus you would use to measure the height of this houseplant.

Estimate how much water it would need. _____

Explain why it would need this much water. _____

_____

CHOOSING AMOUNTS

Investigating how much water seedlings need.

■ Draw your seedling.

How much water will you give it? _____

How often will you water it? _____

What will you use to measure your seedling's height? _____

_____

Where will you measure to? _____

Write a sentence saying how much water is best for seedlings.

_____

_____

SUNDIALS

MATHS FOCUS: UNDERSTAND AND COMPARE ANGLES AS A MEASURE OF TURN

Learning objectives
- To recognise and use whole, half and quarter turns.
- To recognise and make angles greater than/smaller than a quarter turn.

Resources
- Clock faces or dials with moveable hands.
- Card, scissors, paper fasteners.
- Copies of photocopiable pages 36 (page 37 for less able children) and 38.

Introduction
5 mins
- Ask the children to suggest a range of different things that turn round (such as the hands on a clock, wheels on a toy car, or control dials on household appliances). Talk about 'angle' as a way of saying how much something has turned.

Whole-class, teacher-directed activity
10–15 mins
- Show the children a clock face. Ask: *Do you know the names of any angles?* Move the clock hand through a full turn, then a half turn and a quarter turn, making sure the children know the names of these angles. *What is another name for a quarter turn?* (A right angle.) Check that the children know which direction is clockwise and which is anticlockwise.
- Ask individual children to turn a clock hand, or the pointer on a dial, by given amounts (a quarter turn, a half turn, an angle that is more than a quarter turn and less than a half turn). For more able children, choose starting points other than the 'straight up' ('12 o'clock' or 'zero') position.

Children's activity
25–30 mins
- Ask the children to make a dial using a copy of photocopiable page 36, by cutting out the cardboard strips and using a paper fastener to attach these to the dial.
- Encourage the children to use the hands on their dial to experiment with quarter, half and intermediate turns, both clockwise and anticlockwise. By using their own dials, children can experience the effect of quarter and half turns from positions other than the '12 o'clock' position.

Differentiation
More able: Children should work in pairs to set each other problems like the extension question on photocopiable page 36.
Less able: Use photocopiable page 37 to practise half and quarter turns only, both clockwise and anticlockwise with one hand always starting from either the 'straight up' or the 'straight down' position.

SCIENCE LINK ACTIVITY

Photocopiable page 38 allows children to practise different-sized turns in relation to a direction compass. This reinforces the maths skill of understanding different-sized angles, and prepares children for science work about shadows cast by the Sun at different times of the day, when the Sun appears to be in different positions in the sky.

Plenary
10 mins
- Show the children a clock face, and ask them to work out which number the big hand will point to if it turns, for example, *A quarter turn starting from number 2.* Use different starting points and both clockwise and anticlockwise turns, allowing children to use the dials they made in the children's activity if necessary. Show the children a range of card strips, opened to different size angles between 0° and 180°. Can the children put them in order of size?

SUNDIALS

SCIENCE FOCUS: LIGHT AND SHADOWS (QCA UNIT 3F)

Learning objective
- To know that shadows change length and position throughout the day.
- To measure the length of a shadow in standard units.

Resources
- Blu-Tack, pencil, torch.
- Sticks held upright in small pots of damp sand (one stick per pair or small group), chalk, metre rulers, a direction compass, a bright, sunny day!
- Copies of photocopiable page 39.
  Ideally the whole-class activity should be done before the children's activity, to give the children an understanding of how the Sun moves over an entire day before they start making their own sundial.

Introduction
5 mins
- Recap the children's knowledge of shadows. They should know they only have a shadow when it is sunny. Some children may be aware that the position of their shadow changes during the day.

Whole-class, teacher-directed activity
15–20 mins
- Discuss the children's ideas about whether or not the Sun's position moves during the day. Some children may be aware that shadows are in different places in the morning and the evening, but the majority probably won't know. (Try placing cut-out yellow circles on the classroom window at hourly intervals throughout the day to show how the position of the Sun in the sky seems to change.)
- Use a pencil held upright in a lump of Blu-Tack and a torch to explore how shadows move when the light comes from different directions. Many children will not be aware that a shadow is on the opposite side of an object from the light source, so spend plenty of time on establishing this point.
- Hold an unlit torch in different positions around the pencil and ask the children to predict where the shadow will be. Switch on the torch to see if they were correct.

Children's activity
20–25 mins
- Children should work in pairs or small groups to build their own sundial, based on the instructions on photocopiable page 39. (You will need to check that the area of playground you choose remains in sunlight throughout the school day.)
- With their sundials set up, the children should mark the length and direction of the shadow at regular intervals throughout the day. In one hour the shadow will have moved 15° – far enough for the children not to confuse adjacent positions. A large set of compass directions drawn on the playground will help children decide on the direction of their shadows.
- Ask the children to complete the questions on photocopiable page 39.

Differentiation
More able: Ask the children to relate the length of a shadow to the position of the Sun in the sky. (At midday the Sun is high in the sky so the shadow is short; when the Sun is lower in the sky the shadow is longer.)
Less able: Ask these children to model the effect they see in the playground, using an upright pencil and a torch. Can they work out why the shadow in the playground moves?

Links to other topics
History: How did ancient people tell the time? Children might enjoy hiding the classroom clock for a day and telling the time from the Sun's position in the sky!

Different size angles

■ Cut out some hands. Use a paper fastener to make a dial.

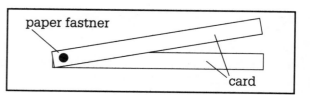

paper fastner

card

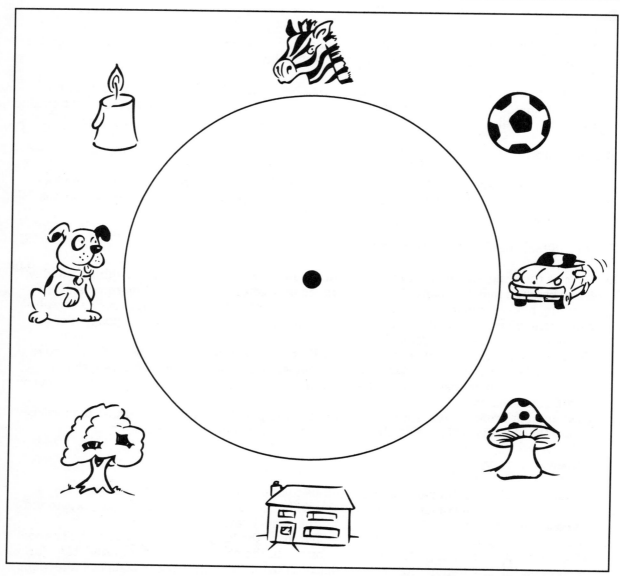

■ Point one hand at the zebra. Turn the other hand a quarter turn clockwise. What does it point to?

■ Find other pairs of pictures using a quarter turn. Write them down on the back of the sheet. Put the starting point picture first. Say whether the turn was clockwise or anticlockwise.

■ Find pairs of pictures for a turn that is bigger than a quarter turn and smaller than a half turn. Write the pairs down on the back of the sheet.

NOW TRY THIS If you start at the zebra, how far do you have to turn one hand clockwise so that it points to the tree? Make up more questions for your partner.

Clockwise and anticlockwise

■ Cut out some hands. Use a paper fastener to make a dial.

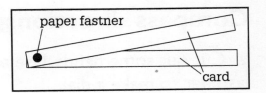

■ Point one hand at the zebra. Turn the other hand. On the back of the sheet, write down what it points to after turning:
- ▪ a quarter turn clockwise
- ▪ a quarter turn anticlockwise.

■ Point one hand at the house. Turn the other hand and write down what it points to after turning:
- ▪ a quarter turn anticlockwise
- ▪ a quarter turn clockwise.

NOW TRY THIS Find pairs of pictures that are a half turn apart.

SHAPE AND SPACE PHOTOCOPIABLE

Compass directions

Cut out some hands. Use a paper fastener to make a dial.

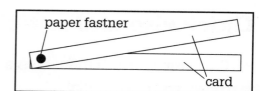

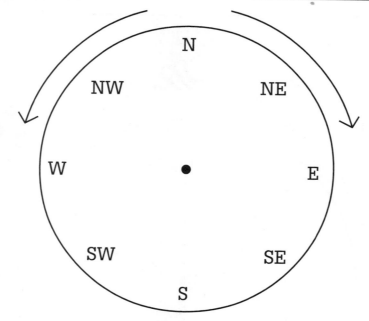

Point one hand to north on the compass. Turn the other hand and fill in the table to show the direction it points in.

Amount second hand is turned	Where it points to
Half a turn anticlockwise	
Less than a quarter turn clockwise	
More than a quarter and less than a half turn anticlockwise	
Quarter turn clockwise	
Less than a quarter turn anticlockwise	
More than a quarter and less than a half turn clockwise	
Quarter turn anticlockwise	

Making a sundial

■ Put a stick in a sunny spot in the playground to make your own sundial. Make sure it's in a safe, sunny place.

■ Use chalk to mark the position of the shadow every hour.

■ Record the length of the shadow in a table like this:

Time	Length of shadow

■ Plot a bar chart to show how the length of the shadow changes during the day.

When is the shadow shortest? _____

When do you think it will be longest? _____

What happens to the position of the shadow during the day? _____

_____

Explain this by saying how the Sun seems to move each day. _____

_____

Which way does the shadow point at midday? _____

FOOD SURVEY

MATHS FOCUS: USING CARROLL DIAGRAMS

Learning objectives
- To classify according to one criterion.
- To represent a classification as a Carroll diagram.

Resources
- Copies of a school meals menu.
- Copies of photocopiable pages 42 (page 43 for less able children) and 44, copies of resource page 126 (including A3 copies).

Introduction
5 mins
- Explain that this lesson is about sorting things out according to one criterion or characteristic. Tell the children that they can already do this very well – prove it with some examples: *Put your hand up if you are a boy. Put your hand up if you are not a boy. Put your hand up if you like apples. Put your hand up if you don't like apples.*

Whole class, teacher directed activity
15 mins
- Show the children the top half of the enlarged copy of resource page 126. Explain: *This is a Carroll diagram that we can use to show how we sort things.*
- Write 'Children in our class' as the title, then 'Boys' and 'Not boys' at the top of the columns. Help the children to decide where some of their names should be written. Write them in.
- Uncover the lower half of resource page 126. Write 'Children in our class' again in the title box, 'Boys' inside the circle and 'Not boys' outside the circle. Ask the children decide where some names should be written, and write them in. Help them to understand that this is just a different way of showing the same information as in the top Carroll diagram.
- Repeat the activity on another enlarged copy of the sheet to produce Carroll diagrams representing the information about liking apples.

Children's activity
25–30 mins
- Working in groups on photocopiable page 42, ask the children to sort out who in their group has a school lunch, who has a packed lunch and who goes home.
  - Using this information, ask the groups to make two different Carroll diagrams on a copy of resource page 126, according to the criteria listed on the worksheet.

SCIENCE LINK ACTIVITY

This activity should follow a class discussion about different food groups. Provide small groups of children with a copy of a school meals menu, and a copy each of photocopiable pages 44 and 126. Ask them to make Carroll diagrams grouping the foods on the school menu into four main groups – 'meat and fish', 'fats', 'starches and sugars' and 'fruit and vegetables'. Encourage them to think about whether any menu items, for example sausage rolls, contain more than one type of food.

Differentiation
More able: Ask the children if they could use the diagrams to find the total number of children in their group. *Does everybody's name appear on the Carroll diagrams? Why not?* (The diagram doesn't include all the children – in this case, those who go home for lunch.)

Less able: Use copies of photocopiable sheet 43, which shows the Carroll diagrams with titles already written on.

Plenary
10 mins
- Discuss the two types of Carroll diagram the children have created. Does each show the same amount of information? Ask volunteers to say which type they find easier to make and easier to understand and why.

SCIENCE FOCUS: TEETH AND EATING (QCA UNIT 3A)

Learning objectives
■ To know that all animals, including humans, need to feed, and their 'diet' describes what they eat.
■ To know that animals need to feed to grow and to be active.

Resources
■ Board or flip chart, marker pens, pictures or examples of food packaging for a wide range of different foods (baked beans, chips, sausages, milk, sugar, cheese and so on).
■ Copies of photocopiable pages 45 and 126.
This lesson could form part of follow-up work after a visit to a local supermarket to look at the range of foods available. Consult your school/LEA guidelines about any off-site visits.

Introduction
5 mins
Write the word 'diet' on the board. *Who can read this word? Who can explain what it means?* Discuss 'diet' as a description of all the food that a person (or animal) eats – most children will only have heard about 'diet' in the context of a slimming diet.

Whole-class, teacher-directed activity
10–15 mins
■ Ask the children what they think is meant by a 'balanced diet'. Most children will have some idea because they will be aware that just eating sweets 'isn't good for you'. Discuss the idea of a healthy diet being one that contains a wide range of different foods, including all the different types of food you need.
■ Introduce the children to the main food groups: 'meat, fish and pulses', 'fats', 'starches and sugars' and 'fruit and vegetables'. Write these as list headings on the board. Ask the children to find examples of foods from each of the groups, explaining that 'starches and sugars' includes both sweet foods and stodgy foods (foods that make you feel full, like bread, biscuits, rice and potatoes).
■ Discuss why it is important to eat foods from all the different food groups, concentrating on the idea that foods help you grow – 'foods for growth' – and give you energy – 'foods for activity'. Give examples of foods that fall into these groups.

Children's activity
20–25 mins
■ Working in small groups, ask the children to complete the first part of photocopiable page 45. They should then use food packaging to help them find examples of 'foods for growth' (such as fish fingers) and 'foods for activity' (such as chips), adding these to the lists on the worksheet. They should then present these in the form of Carroll diagrams, either drawing their own or using the templates on page 126.

Differentiation
More able: Ask the children to compare the 'foods for growth' and 'foods for activity' with the foods in the four main food groups that they listed on the board earlier. Can they spot any general pattern? (Generally meat, fish and pulses are 'foods for growth', starches and sugar are 'foods for activity'. Fats, like cheese and dairy products can be in both groups.)
Less able: The children may need support with the concepts of 'foods for growth' and 'foods for activity', and help with grouping foods accordingly. Ask the children: *Do you know which foods are 'good for you'?* (Foods for growth.) *Which foods make you feel 'full up'?* (Foods for activity.)

Links to other topics
Design and technology: Make healthy and unhealthy snack foods. **Art:** Make posters or menus advertising different foods. **Literacy:** Write instructions or recipes for different snack foods.
PSHE: Write a well-being plan based around a healthy diet and exercise (activity).

FOOD SURVEY

Carroll diagrams

■ Write the names of children in your group in the correct column.

Children who go home to lunch	Children who have school dinners	Children who have a packed lunch

■ Use the top diagram on the 'Carroll diagrams' sheet.
■ Write the title 'Children who have dinner at school'.
■ Sort the children in your group into two categories: 'Have packed lunches' and 'Don't have packed lunches'.
■ Fill in the Carroll diagram.

■ On the bottom diagram on the 'Carroll diagrams' sheet, write the title 'Children who have dinner at school'.
■ Complete the Carroll diagram to show the children who have packed lunches.

NOW TRY THIS Were all the children in your group included in both Carroll diagrams? Which children would not be included?

Carroll diagrams

■ Tick the sentence that is correct for you.

I go home for lunch. ☐

I have a school dinner. ☐

I have a packed lunch. ☐

■ Write the names of the children in your group in this Carroll diagram.

Children who have lunch at school	
Have a packed lunch	**Don't have a packed lunch**

■ Now write your group's names in this Carroll diagram

Children who have lunch at school

Don't have a packed lunch

Have a packed lunch

NOW TRY THIS Were all the children in your group included in both Carroll diagrams? Which children would not be included?

FOOD SURVEY

Our school meals

■ List as many foods as you can from your school meal menu.

■ Draw four Carroll diagrams to show foods that are:
- Meat and fish / Not meat and fish
- Fats / Not fats
- Starches and sugars / Not starches and sugars
- Fruit and vegetables / Not fruit and vegetables.

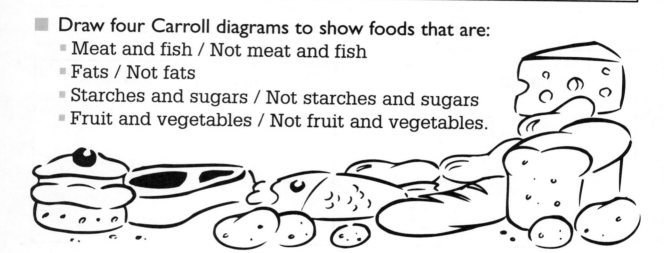

■ The lists below show you some examples of food in each of the different food groups.

Meat, fish and pulses	Fats	Starches and sugars	Fruit and vegetables
Tuna	Cheese	Bread	Apple
Bacon	Butter	Rice	Carrot
Beefburger	Margarine	Potato	Orange
Fish fingers	Ice cream	Cake	Onion
	Olive oil	Sweet foods	

NOW TRY THIS Are there any foods that could go in more than one group? For example a sausage roll could go in both the 'meat and fish' and 'starches and sugars' categories.

Food survey

■ Write down two examples of each of these food types.

Meat and fish _____

Fats _____

Starches and sugars _____

Fruit and vegetables _____

■ Write a sentence to say why you should eat a balanced diet.

■ Some foods help you grow. Draw a Carroll diagram showing 'Foods for growth' and 'Not foods for growth'. The list below gives you some examples.

■ Some foods give you energy. Draw a Carroll diagram showing 'Foods for activity' and 'Not foods for activity'. The list below gives you some examples.

Foods for growth	Foods for activity
Meat	Bread
Fish	Potatoes
Cheese	Pasta
Lentils	Biscuits
Beans	Cakes
Eggs	Sweet foods

What types of food are good for helping you grow?

CLASSIFYING WITH VENN DIAGRAMS

MATHS FOCUS: CLASSIFYING OBJECTS

Learning objectives
- To classify objects or shapes according to one, then two criteria.
- To display classification on a Venn diagram.

Resources
- A selection of pencils (including writing and colouring pencils, some sharpened, some not)
- A selection of regular and non-regular 2-D shapes, Post-it Notes, Blu-Tack, scissors, glue.
- Copies of photocopiable pages 48 (page 49 for less able children) and 50 on coloured paper. Enlarged copies of resource page 127 on white paper, plus one large class copy.

Introduction
5 mins
- Tell the children that we sort things out all the time. Show them the collection of pencils and ask: *How could we sort these into two groups?* Children might suggest sorting them into 'coloured' and 'writing', or into 'needs sharpening' and 'doesn't need sharpening'. Sort the pencils as they suggest, then show (or ask them to show) another way of sorting the pencils.

Whole class, teacher-directed activity
10–15 mins
- Using the class copy of resource page 127, show the children the top diagram. Explain: *This is a Venn diagram. We can use it to show how we have sorted things.*
- Look at the selection of 2-D shapes and ask the children to decide on one criterion by which to sort them (such as *straight edges* or *number of sides*). Use Post-it Notes to label the top diagram ('straight edges' inside the circle and 'not straight edges' outside, for example). Sort the shapes by the chosen criterion, and stick them to the sheet with Blu-Tack.
- Now choose a second criterion as well. Look at diagram 2 on the class copy of the resource sheet, and label the two circles ('straight edges' and 'four sides', for example). Sort the shapes again, this time using both criteria and stick them to the appropriate part of the Venn diagram. Make sure the children understand that the shapes with 'straight edges' *and* 'four sides' should be placed where the circles overlap.

Children's activity
20–25 mins
- Give each child copies of photocopiable pages 48 and 127. Ask them to cut out the shapes and sort them using the 'Venn diagram' sheet according to a single criterion of their choice. When they have sorted the shapes, they should stick them to the sheet.
- Then ask them to sort the same shapes by two criteria, drawing them in the correct places on the lower half of the resource sheet.

Differentiation
More able: Ask the children to extend the number of shapes in each group by drawing an extra shape with the appropriate criterion.
Less able: Use photocopiable page 49 for this activity. This practises grouping according to one criterion only, so children will only need the top Venn diagram from resource page 127.

SCIENCE LINK ACTIVITY

Photocopiable page 50 shows a selection of shells, with suggestions for some grouping criteria that the children could use. Ask the children to group the shells according to one of these, or according to a criterion of their own. Use resource page 127 to display their groupings.

Plenary
10 mins
- Look at some of the ways by which the children grouped their objects. Cover the labels on the Venn diagrams and ask other children to identify the groupings chosen. Show the children a 2-D shape from your selection – can anybody put it in the correct section of the Venn diagram?

SCIENCE FOCUS: ROCKS AND SOILS (QCA UNIT 3D)

Learning objectives
- To observe and compare rocks.
- To know that rocks can be grouped according to observable characteristics.

Resources
- Samples of different types of rock, (different-sized samples of the same type of rock are helpful), a hammer and safety screen.
- Blunt metal knives or scrapers, hand lenses.
- Copies of photocopiable page 51, A3 copies of resource page 127, stuck to card to give extra strength, Blu-Tack.

Safety: If you use a hammer to break rocks, wear eye protection and use a plastic screen to protect children from possible flying fragments.

Introduction
5 mins
- Show the children a selection of different-sized rock samples: *What are these?* Discuss when we use the words 'rock' 'stone' and 'pebble', and the relative difference in their size. Look at samples that are clearly the same type of rock, but are different sizes. Explain that the same type of rock can be described as rock, stones or pebbles. (You could use a hammer to break a sample into smaller pieces to show this is the case.)

Whole-class, teacher-directed activity
10 mins
- Ask the children to describe some of the rock samples you have. Encourage a range of vocabulary about size, shape, texture and colour.
- Ask: *Who can suggest a way of sorting these rocks into two groups?* Sort the rocks according to one of the groupings suggested. Choose samples small enough to stick with Blu-Tack to the top Venn diagram on resource page 127.
- Encourage the children to suggest other ways of grouping the rock samples, asking them to select samples that would fit into each of the groupings they suggest.
- Remind the children of how to use a Venn diagram to sort things by more than one criterion.
- Show the children how to rub rocks with a blunt knife or scraper to test if they are soft or hard. Introduce words such as 'grainy' 'sandy' and 'crumbly' to describe rocks that wear away easily.

Children's activity
20–25 mins
- In groups, ask the children to examine a selection of rock samples carefully and describe some ways in which they differ, then sort the samples according to either one or two criteria.
- Photocopiable page 51 gives some suggested groupings, but children can chose their own.
- The children should display their results by placing their rock samples onto one of the Venn diagrams on an enlarged copy of resource page 127.

Differentiation
More able: Ask the children to group their rocks according to two criteria. Encourage them to use hand lenses to observe the rocks carefully and compare the sizes of the particles. If possible, provide simple secondary sources that the children can use to identify one or two rock types.

Less able: Give children one simple criterion by which to group their rocks (such as pebbles/not pebbles or smooth/not smooth). Use only the top Venn diagram from resource page 127.

Links to other topics
Geography: Can the children remember holidays with sandy beaches or stony beaches? Look at pictures of beaches from different places. **Art:** Look at stone statues. Use simple sculpting tools to make statues out of clay or salt dough.

CLASSIFYING WITH VENN DIAGRAMS

Sorting shapes using venn diagrams

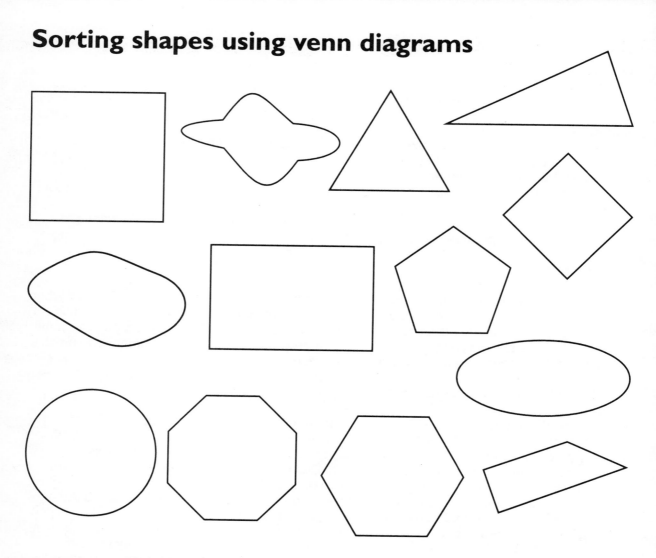

■ Cut out these shapes.

■ Choose **one** of the following criteria:
- shapes with straight sides
- shapes with three sides
- shapes that are rectangles
- shapes with all sides the same length.

■ Label the top Venn diagram on the 'Venn diagram' sheet.

■ Sort the shapes according to your chosen criterion, and stick them in the correct places on the top Venn diagram.

■ Now label the circles on the bottom Venn diagram with 'straight sides' and 'four sides'.

■ Stick the shapes in the correct places on Venn diagram 2.

NOW TRY THIS   Draw one more shape that goes in each section of Venn diagram 2.

CLASSIFYING WITH VENN DIAGRAMS

Making a Venn diagram

■ Cut out these shapes.

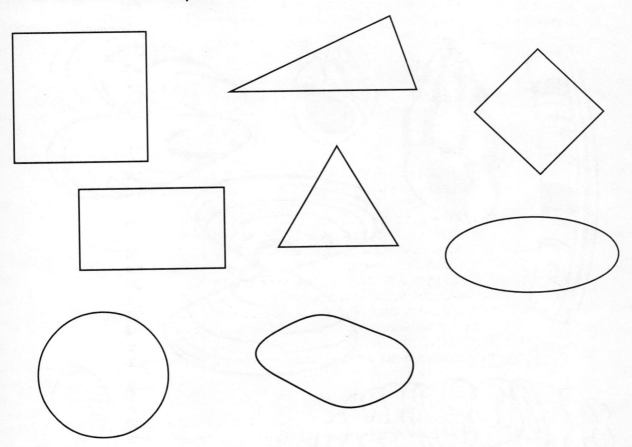

■ Label the top Venn diagram on the 'Venn diagram' worksheet like this:

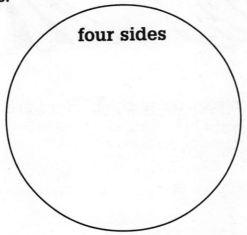

four sides

■ Stick the shapes in the correct places.

NOW TRY THIS Can you think of a different way to sort these shapes using a Venn diagram?

CLASSIFYING WITH VENN DIAGRAMS

Venn diagrams of shells

Here are some shells Jyoti found on the beach.

■ Make a Venn diagram to sort these shells. Here are some suggestions of how you could sort the shells:

- has two parts
- has a point
- is rounded.

■ Cut out the shells and stick them on the top Venn diagram on your 'Venn diagram' sheet. Could you make a Venn diagram using two criteria? Try sorting the shells using the bottom Venn diagram on the sheet.

Sorting rocks

■ Use a hand lens to examine your rock samples.

■ Write six words you could use to describe the rocks.

_____   _____

_____   _____

_____   _____

■ Now sort your rocks using one or two criteria. Choose from this list, or make up your own:
  ▪ pebbles
  ▪ smooth
  ▪ grainy or sandy
  ▪ crumbly
  ▪ rough edges
  ▪ yellowy.

■ Make a Venn diagram to show how you sorted the rocks.

NOW TRY THIS   Could you sort your rocks to make a different Venn diagram?

HANDLING AND INTERPRETING DATA

CHOOSE THE BEST

MATHS FOCUS: USING FREQUENCY TABLES

Learning objectives
- To solve a given problem by collecting, sorting and organising information.
- To make and interpret a frequency table.

Resources
- Board or flip chart, marker pens.
- Copies of photocopiable pages 60 (page 61 for less able children) and 62.

Introduction
5 mins
- Draw a frequency table on the board and write 'frequency table' as a heading.
- Tell the children: *We use a frequency table to find out 'how many'*. Give examples, such as 'How many pencils we can hold', or 'How many children like different colours'. Ask the class to suggest some more examples.

Whole-class, teacher-directed activity
10–15 mins
- Tell the children: *We are going to find out how popular different pop groups are.* (You could use films, videos, books or football teams if this would be more appropriate for your children.) Make sure they understand that 'how popular' means how many people like them.
- Ask children to name some (no more than four or five) of their favourite pop groups. List them in the frequency table on the board.
- Tell the children that they must vote *once* only for their favourite from the list on the board, using a show of hands. Write the votes in the frequency table next to each pop group.
- Help the children to use the information to answer questions, such as: *Which group is most popular/did most children like? How many children liked (a pop group) best? Name a group that got more votes than (a pop group).*

Children's activity
25–30 mins
- Photocopiable page 60 suggests some questions children can find out about using frequency tables. Working in groups, ask the children to choose a topic (either from the worksheet or of their own choosing), decide what information to collect, then collect the relevant information, fill in the frequency table on the worksheet and use this to answer questions.
- Tell the children to work in pairs within their groups to set and answer more questions about their frequency table.
- Each group should choose one person to report back to the class about what they did and what they found out.

Differentiation
More able: For the topic they looked at, ask children to think about who might find the information useful and why. Think of some more people who might use frequency tables. What would they use them for?

Less able: Use photocopiable page 61. Children should work in pairs to complete the sheet.

SCIENCE LINK ACTIVITY

Photocopiable page 62 shows the results, in picture form, of an activity to investigate how many spoonfuls of water different materials could hold. Ask the children to use these results to make a frequency table for the different materials, then use the table to answer questions about possible uses for the materials.

Plenary
10 mins
- Ask one person from each group to report back to the class. Can they suggest a use for the information they have found out?
  Encourage other children in the group and the class to help. Talk about whether the results for any of the topics might change if the activity was done by a different group of children (Year 6, for example).

CHOOSE THE BEST

SCIENCE FOCUS: CHARACTERISTICS OF MATERIALS (QCA UNIT 3C)

Learning objectives
■ To plan and carry out a test safely.
■ To use results to make comparisons and draw conclusions.

Resources
■ A selection of different cleaning cloths (or materials that might be used as cleaning cloths), blocks of wood to wrap the cloths around, access to hard surfaces such as brick or concrete.
■ Copies of photocopiable page 63.

Safety: Make sure the children know that they should wrap the cloth round the block of wood before they rub it, so they don't graze their fingers on the hard surface.

Introduction
5 mins
■ Show the children your collection of different materials. Ask: *How could we describe the properties of these cloths/materials?* (Possibilities include softness, fluffiness, smoothness, absorbency, durability, tear resistance, fray resistance, thickness, coarseness and so on).

Whole-class, teacher-directed activity
10–15 mins
■ Ask the children what properties they think a cleaning cloth should have. If they do not include durability ('how hard-wearing it is' or 'how long it will last'), then lead them to consider this.
■ Ask: *How could we test how hard-wearing a cloth is, or how long it lasts?* Help the children to plan an investigation into this, emphasising the importance of fair testing. Discuss what they should change (the type of cloth) and what they should keep the same (the surface they rub on, how hard they rub, the thickness of the cloth they use and so on).
■ Decide how to record the results – a frequency table showing the number of times they have to rub each cloth before wearing a hole in it.

Children's activity
20–25 mins
■ Working in small groups, children should carry out a 'rub test' for each of the different types of cleaning cloth, using photocopiable page 63 to record what they do and the results they obtain.
■ Encourage the groups to think about what they are doing to make the test fair, and about possible ways to improve their investigation.
■ The children should use their frequency table to draw a conclusion, deciding which material/cleaning cloth would last longest, writing their conclusion on the worksheet.

Differentiation
More able: Ask the children: *Is the cloth that lasts longest always the best cleaning cloth?* Ask them to think of other properties that a good cleaning cloth might need. They should recognise that this may depend on what the cloth is used to clean.
Less able: Ask the children to decide whether or not the test they carried out was a fair test, and to list the things they did to make the test fair.

Links to other topics
Literacy: Ask groups to write and perform television or radio advertisements for new cleaning cloths. Ask a panel of 'consumers' to decide which cloth they would buy, and why. **History:** Look at materials used through the ages to make clothing for different situations – what material would they use for a soldier? A farmer? How are they different? Which would they most like to wear?

CHOOSE THE BEST

Making a frequency table

▨ Choose one of these topics to investigate. Tick the topic you choose.

☐ What colours do children in our group like?

☐ How many pencils can our pencil cases hold?

☐ How many pets do children in our group have?

☐ How many nursery rhymes do children in our group know?

☐ How do children in our group travel to school?

▨ Make a frequency table to find out about your topic. Give it a heading.

	How many children

What does your frequency table tell you?

NOW TRY THIS   Who might find this information useful? Why?

Making a frequency table

We are going to find out about (tick **one** topic)

☐ What colours do children in our group like?

☐ How children in our group travel to school

■ Write either **Colours** or **Ways to travel** as a heading in the top row of your frequency table.

■ List four colours **or** four ways to travel to school in the first column of the frequency table.

	How many children

■ Now find out how many children like each colour, **or** find out how many children use each way to travel to school.

■ Write the numbers in the second column of the frequency table.

■ Complete this sentence:

Most children in our group _____

_____

_____

CHOOSE THE BEST

Which material holds most water?

Class 3 tested different materials by pouring water on them.
They counted how many spoonfuls of water the material held before
it dripped.

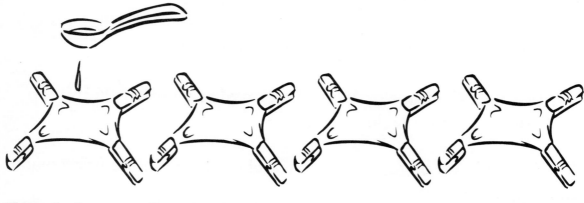

Flannel – 8   Smooth cotton – 3   Nylon – 1   Kitchen towel – 5

■ Make a frequency table to show these results.

Type of material	How many spoonfuls

Which material would you use to make a towel? Why?

Which material would you use to make an umbrella? Why?

MATHS SKILLS FOR SCIENCE: YEARS 3&4

CHOOSE THE BEST

The rub test

■ Complete this sentence.
We used a rub test to find out _____

_____

■ Make a frequency table to show your results.

Which cloth would last longest?

■ List the things you did to make it a fair test.

How could you improve this test?

NOW TRY THIS Are there any other properties that a good cleaning cloth might need?

FOOD PREFERENCES

MATHS FOCUS: PRESENTING AND INTERPRETING DATA

Learning objectives
- To collect data and make a frequency table.
- To represent data as a pictogram or bar chart.
- To use pictograms or bar charts to answer questions and solve problems.

Resources
- Pieces of four different types of freshly prepared fruit (ideally apple, strawberry, grape, banana, but this could vary depending on the season) – enough of each fruit for just over a quarter of the children in the class.
- Board or flip chart, marker pens.
- Photocopiable pages 54 (page 55 for less able children), 56 and resource page 124 or 125.

Hygiene: Ensure that all food and dishes are scrupulously clean. Children should wash their hands at the start of the lesson. You could use pictures or coloured buttons instead of real fruit.

Introduction
5 mins
- Explain to the children that, as a class, you are going to investigate the types of fruit they like best and explore whether or not the results you get are accurate.
- Offer round the prepared fruit, each labelled with its name or a picture. Ask each child to take one piece of the fruit they like best, remembering what they choose. Don't force children to choose if they don't like any of those on offer – just discount these from the data.

Whole-class, teacher-directed activity
10 mins
- Use a show of hands to find out how many children chose each type of fruit. Record this information on the board in a class frequency table.
- Ask the children to suggest other ways of presenting the same information. If necessary, guide them towards bar charts and pictograms. Recap how to make each of these.

Children's activity
20–25 mins
- Ask groups to present the information from the frequency table as either a pictogram (using resource page 125) or a bar chart (using resource page 124).
- Use photocopiable page 54 to guide group discussion about how good the evidence is, and whether results might change in other circumstances. The survey doesn't really show what fruit we like because there are only four choices. Children should realise that results are not always accurate, even if they are collected carefully.

Differentiation
More able: Ask the children to suggest what conclusions they can draw from these results, and how they might be improved.

Less able: Use photocopiable page 55 and provide help where necessary.

SCIENCE LINK ACTIVITY

Photocopiable page 56 can be used to introduce an investigation into what food dogs like. Children can use the data to practise plotting a bar chart or pictogram in the space on the worksheet. Encourage each group to discuss whether the information collected presents an accurate picture of dogs' favourite food, and if not, why not. ('My dog might like tinned food best, but we only give him dried food.')

Plenary
10 mins
- Look at the frequency table, and the children's bar charts and pictograms. Notice that each chart shows the same thing but in a different way.
- Ask: *Do these results really show what fruit we like best, or were any problems?* ('I like apple best, but there wasn't any left' or 'I like pears best, but there weren't any'.)

SCIENCE FOCUS: TEETH AND EATING (QCA UNIT 3A)

Learning objectives
- To turn ideas about the diet of animals into a form that can be investigated.
- To present evidence about the food eaten by animals in a bar chart or pictogram.
- To decide whether evidence is sufficient to draw conclusions.

Resources
- A selection of labels or pictures from a range of different cat foods.
- Copies of photocopiable page 57 and resource pages 124 and 125.

Preparation: You may find it convenient to do the teacher-directed activity and the children's activity on separate days, possibly asking the children to collect data about their own pet's diet as a homework activity.

Introduction
5 mins
- Look at the labels from the different cat foods. Ask: *Who has a cat? Does it eat foods like any of these?* Allow children to comment on the food their cat eats, how often they feed it, how much and so on. *What food does your cat like best?* Children who don't own pets could consider questions like: *What sort of food do pets eat? Do they all eat the same sort of food?*

Whole-class, teacher-directed activity
10–15 mins
- Explain that you would like the children to find out something about the food their cats, or other pets (choose the most appropriate animal to focus on according to your class) like to eat. Help them to think of questions they could investigate, such as *Do all cats eat the same food? What food do cats like best?*, then choose one question to answer as a class.
- Help the children to decide on what information they will need to answer the class question (here, a record of the type of food eaten by all the children's cats on one particular day).
- Discuss how the different types of food could be described (perhaps fresh food, tinned food, dried food). Children may want to include all the different makes and flavours of tinned food, for example, but at this stage it's best to stick to broad categories, otherwise you could end up with 28 different results! Help the children to decide how many types of food they can collect evidence for, and how to categorise all the different types of food available.
- Ask the children to think about ways of presenting the results once they have been collected. Children without pets could think about what food they would give a pet if they had one.

Children's activity
20–25 mins
- The children should work in groups, using a copy of photocopiable page 57 to decide how to present the information about cats' diets. This can be as a pictogram (using resource page 125), or as a bar chart (using resource page 124).
- Encourage the children to think about how good their evidence is: *Were there enough animals included in the survey? How many would be enough? What conclusions can you draw?* (With a sample this small, it's unlikely there will be enough evidence for the children to draw conclusions.) It's important for children to learn that sometimes the evidence is insufficient to draw reliable conclusions.

Differentiation
More able: Consider whether there are ways that they could change the investigation so it gives a more reliable conclusion. (They could ask all the children in the school, or give the cats a choice of two foods.)
Less able: Help the children, if necessary, to construct their pictogram or bar chart.

Links to other topics
History: Look at life in medieval times and earlier – why did people keep cats then? **Literacy:** Write leaflets or instructions about 'How to look after my pet while I am on holiday' or 'How I will look after my friend's pet while they're on holiday'.

FOOD PREFERENCES

What fruit do we like?

■ Fill in the frequency table to show which fruit everybody chose.

Type of fruit	How many children
Apple	
Strawberry	
Grape	
Banana	

■ Using another sheet, draw a bar chart or a pictogram to show how many children chose each type of fruit.

How many children chose grape? _____

Which fruit did most children choose? _____

How many children chose this fruit? _____

How many children altogether chose fruit? _____

Do you think this shows the fruit children in your class like best? Discuss this in your group.

NOW TRY THIS   How could you improve this investigation?

FOOD PREFERENCES

What fruit do we like?

■ Fill in the frequency table to show which fruit everybody chose.

Type of fruit	How many children
Apple	
Strawberry	
Grape	
Banana	

■ On another sheet, draw a bar chart or a pictogram of the results.

Which fruit did most children choose? _____

Which fruit did least children choose? _____

Which fruit did you choose? Is it your favourite fruit? _____

_____

_____

Do your results show the fruit children in your class like best?
Talk about it in your group.

Types of dog food

Class 3 collected information to show what kind of food their pet dogs ate. This is what they found out.

Type of food	How many dogs eat it
Dried food	7
Fresh meat	2
Tinned food	5
Puppy food	1

■ Draw a bar chart or a pictogram of this information in the space below.

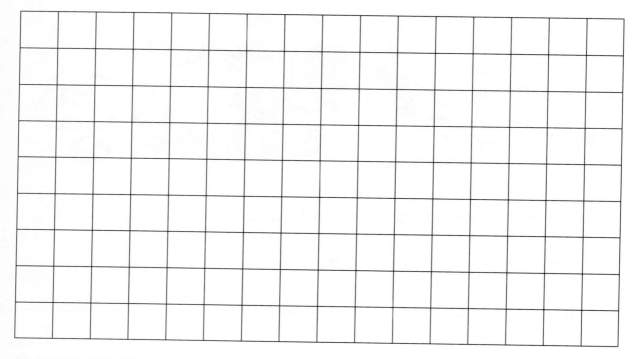

What food did most dogs eat? _____

Do you think dogs like this food best? Discuss in your groups.

Write one sentence to say what you decided. _____

_____

FOOD PREFERENCES

Investigating pets' diets

■ What question you will investigate? _____

_____

_____

■ What information will you collect? Record it in this space.

_____

■ On another sheet of paper, draw a bar chart or pictogram.

What have you found out? _____

_____

_____

What conclusion can you make, if any? _____

_____

_____

_____

NOW TRY THIS Could you change the investigation to improve it?

WHAT DO BAR CHARTS SHOW?

MATHS FOCUS: MAKING BAR CHARTS

Learning objectives

- To solve a problem by collecting and organising information.
- To make a simple bar chart, either by hand or by using a computer.
- To use a bar chart to answer questions.

Resources

- A computer and a simple graphing program that can display data (or an enlarged copy of resource page 124), pencils of different lengths and various colours.
- Board or flip chart, marker pens, 30cm rulers.
- Copies of photocopiable pages 66–8 and resource page 124.

Introduction
5 mins

- Use a show of hands to collect information about the children's favourite colours and record this on the board as a frequency table.

Whole-class, teacher-directed activity
10–15 mins

- Ask a volunteer to explain how we might present the information in the frequency table as a bar chart. Other children can suggest what should go on the axes and how to enter the data.
- Show the children how to enter the information from the frequency table into a graphing program to produce a bar chart on the computer.
- Look at the collection of coloured pencils. Ask: *How could we use this program to draw a bar chart showing how long our coloured pencils are?* Help the children decide what information they would have to collect, how to group the pencils into different lengths, how to record this in a frequency table, and how to enter the information into the graphing program.

Children's activity
25–30 mins

- Give each group of children a selection of pencils that are the same colour but different lengths. Using photocopiable page 66, the children should measure the length of each pencil to the nearest centimetre, recording the measurement in the tally chart.
- When they have measured all the pencils, ask the children to produce a frequency table. Then ask them to enter this information into a graphing program on the computer to plot a bar chart of frequency against length for their colour of pencil, remembering to choose an appropriate title. (Use copies of photocopiable page 67 if you don't have enough computers.)
  - Having plotted their bar chart, ask the children to complete the conclusion on photocopiable page 66.

Differentiation

More able: Use copies of resource page 124 to experiment with marking the vertical axis in ones, twos and fives. Encourage the children to decide which is the best for their data.

Less able: Give children support at the computer if they are using an unfamiliar program. Encourage them to explain what they are doing at each stage, to help their understanding.

SCIENCE LINK ACTIVITY

Photocopiable page 68 shows several members of a family. Ask the children to use a computer to plot a bar chart of height against age, then to try to identify patterns from the bar chart. They should notice that children get taller as they get older, but that grown-ups can be lots of different heights.

Plenary
10 mins

- Display the bar charts for different coloured pencils. For each colour, work out the most common length: 'Most red pencils are less than 5cm long.' Help the children think of possible reasons for differences they find: 'Red pencils are shortest because we use them most often.'

SCIENCE FOCUS: HELPING PLANTS GROW WELL (QCA UNIT 3B)

Learning objectives
- To recognise that plant growth is affected by temperature.
- To recognise when a comparison of plant growth is unfair.
- To know that using just one plant in each set of conditions does not give sufficient evidence.

Resources
- Trays of fast-growing seedlings, such as cress, access to three places at different temperatures (for example, outside, room temperature and near a heater), 15 or 30cm rulers.
- Copies of photocopiable page 69 and resource page 124.

Introduction
5 mins
- Ask the children: *At what time of year do plants grow best?* Talk about when lawns need cutting, when most plants flower, when fruit and vegetables have grown (thinking about the timing of harvest festivals may help here).
- Discuss with the children why they think plants grow better in spring and summer. *In spring and summer it is warmer / sunnier / less rain / less windy.*

Whole-class, teacher-directed activity
10–15 mins
- Tell the children that you would like them to investigate the effect that warmth has on the way plants grow.
- Ask the children to suggest ways of investigating the effect of warmth. Lead them to suggest that they must alter the temperature in which seedlings grow and measure the height the seedlings reach.
- Discuss how to make sure the test is fair: only the temperature must be changed, everything else must stay the same. Ask children to explain why it would not be a fair test to put plants in a fridge (it is cold *and* dark, so both might be affecting the way the plants grow).
- Let the children set up the experiment with the seedlings. Remind them to keep the soil moist for all plants – if appropriate, you could discuss why this is better than giving all plants the same amount of water each day (in a warm place some of the water may dry up so there is less for the plants).
- Discuss why it is better to use trays of seedlings rather than individual plants. (Individual plants might have died or grown slowly whatever conditions they were in.)

Children's activity
20–25 mins
- Each group of children should measure and record the height of one tray of seedlings kept at one temperature for three weeks at half-weekly intervals. The group should decide whether to measure the height of the tallest, shortest or 'middle-sized' seedling when recording their result. Make sure they realise that if they measure the tallest seedling once they must measure the tallest at all other times as well.
- After all the data has been collected, ask the children to plot a bar chart of the height of seedlings over time. Photocopiable page 69 can be used to help with planning and recording.
- After the children have plotted their graphs (on resource page 124 and/or a computer graphing program if available), use a plenary session to compare the height of the seedlings grown in different conditions and to decide if warmth does affect the way seedlings grow.

Differentiation
More able: Ask the children to think about plants they know and discuss whether the 'best' temperature for growth is the same for all plants.
Less able: Help the children to measure only the tallest seedlings. Provide support as necessary to record results and plot a bar chart.

Links to other topics
Geography: Look at food plants that grow in different parts of the world, and seasonal variations in fresh food available in this country.

WHAT DO BAR CHARTS SHOW?

HANDLING AND INTERPRETING DATA   PHOTOCOPIABLE

How long are our pencils?

Our group measured _____ coloured pencils.

■ Fill in the tally chart for the pencils you measured.

Length of pencil	Tally	Total
Less than 5cm		
5cm to 8cm		
8cm to 11cm		
11cm to 14cm		
Over 14cm		

■ Now fill in this frequency chart.

Length of pencil	Number of pencils
Less than 5cm	
5cm to 8cm	
8cm to 11cm	
11cm to 14cm	
Over 14cm	

■ Use the computer, or a set of axes on paper, to draw a bar chart showing the number of pencils of different lengths.

■ Complete this sentence.

Most _____ pencils were _____ cm long.

NOW TRY THIS   How many pencils were longer than 11cm?

Bar chart to show the length of pencils

■ Use your frequency table to fill in this bar chart.

Bar chart for _____ coloured pencils.

	Less than 5cm	5cm to 8cm	8cm to 11cm	11cm to 14cm	Over 14cm
10					
9					
8					
7					
6					
5					
4					
3					
2					
1					

WHAT DO BAR CHARTS SHOW?

How does height change?

Here are eight members of the Burton family. Their jumpers show their age and their height.

■ Plot a bar chart, either on paper or using a computer, to show how height varies with age for the Burton family.

How old is the shortest person? _____

Is this what you expected? Explain why. _____

_____

_____

NOW TRY THIS What numbers did you use on the vertical axis of your bar chart? Why did you choose these numbers?

WHAT DO BAR CHARTS SHOW?

Does warmth affect plant growth?

■ Draw your investigation.

Where were your seedlings? _____

■ What did you change? What did you keep the same?

Kept the same	Changed

■ Record how the height of your seedlings changed.

Time since investigation started	Height of seedlings

■ Use a computer to draw a bar chart to show how height changed.

Why did you use lots of seedlings? _____

_____

NOW TRY THIS Do you think all plants grow best at the same temperature?

HOW MUCH?

MATHS FOCUS: INVESTIGATING AND SOLVING WORD PROBLEMS

Learning objectives
- To choose appropriate number operations and methods to solve problems.
- To make a general statement, giving examples that satisfy it.

Resources
- Board or flip chart, marker pens.
- Copies of photocopiable pages 72 (page 73 for less able children) and 74.

Introduction
5 mins
- Begin with a question and answer session, giving word problems such as: *A bag of apples costs 20p. A bag of pears costs 25p. How much would a bag of apples and a bag of pears be?*
- Make the problems progressively harder, and tell the children that you don't want the answers, you want to know how to work out the answers, for example: 'Add together the cost of the apples and the pears.'

Whole-class, teacher-directed activity
15 mins
- Write a number on the board. Make a general statement about the number, such as: *Multiplying a number by 3 always gives a bigger answer than adding on 10.* Ask who thinks your statement is correct, then ask for suggestions of how to test this.
- Emphasise that it is easier to prove a statement wrong than right – you need only find *one* example that doesn't fit. Finding one example that fits *does not* prove a statement is true.
- Draw a van on the board, and a series of five or six boxes next to it with different weights (or numbers) written on them. Explain: *The van can only carry 2 boxes. What is the heaviest (and lightest) load it could carry? How many loads can you make that are less than…?* Adjust numbers to suit the children in your class.
- Repeat with other similar examples or different numbers, choosing some that the least able children will be comfortable with, and some that will challenge the more able.

Children's activity
20–25 mins
- Give the children a copy each of photocopiable page 72 and ask them to complete sheet. They should complete the first section individually, but they may benefit from working together to complete the second part of the sheet.
- Most children will probably state that the van can always carry two crates; more able children may say that it is always possible to load three, and sometimes four, crates if you select them carefully.

Differentiation
More able: Ask the children to find all the combinations of three crates that total exactly 600kg (310 + 200 + 90 = 600; 280 + 230 + 90 = 600; 260 + 230 + 110 = 600; 230 + 200 + 170 = 600).

Less able: Use photocopiable page 73, which deals with simpler numbers. (The most crates the van could carry is 4: 250 + 200 + 100 + 50 = 600; 250 + 150 + 100 + 50 = 550, or 200 + 150 + 100 + 50 = 500.)

SCIENCE LINK ACTIVITY

Photocopiable page 74 has a series of problems, introducing the idea that the force required to move something may vary on different surfaces. This links to the science topic of friction, in which children explore why different surfaces require different forces and which surfaces require the largest forces.

Plenary
10 mins
- Ask the children to explain how they decide which number operations to use when they solve word problems. Highlight some of the key words to look for, such as 'How much…', or 'total' for addition, or 'What is the difference…' for subtraction and so on.

SOLVING PROBLEMS

SCIENCE FOCUS: FRICTION (QCA UNIT 4E)

Learning objectives
- To know that there is a force between an object and a surface that may prevent the object moving.
- To use a force meter carefully to measure forces.
- To explain conclusions in terms of the roughness or smoothness of surfaces.

Resources
- Board or flip chart, marker pens.
- Each group will need: a range of different surfaces (for example carpet, vinyl, smooth wood, rough wood, sandpaper; these surfaces could be in the form of sheets that children can hold flat with weights at the corners), wooden blocks or small weighted containers with a means of attaching a force meter (such as a loop of string held on with sticky tape), a force meter.
- Copies of photocopiable page 75 and resource page 124.

Introduction
5 mins
- Ask the children for ideas of things that are slippery and things that aren't. Discuss situations where 'slippery' is fun (skating on ice) or dangerous (wet floors), and where 'not slippery' is useful (goalkeepers' gloves) and a nuisance (slides that 'won't slide').

Whole-class, teacher-directed activity
10–15 mins
- Ask the children to name some surfaces that they think objects will slide over easily, and list them on the board. *Can you spot anything these surfaces have in common?*
- Help them to formulate their ideas as a question that can be tested: 'We think it is easier to slide things on smooth surfaces.' Talk about how the question can be investigated: *What do we need to measure?* If necessary, remind the children of how a force meter can be used to measure how hard it is to pull something along. *What do we need to change? What do we need to keep the same to make sure it is a fair test?*
- Show the children how to compare friction between different surfaces by measuring the force needed to pull a block along each of the different surfaces.

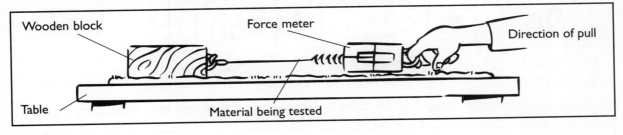

Children's activity
20–25 mins
- Set groups of children the task of comparing the friction between a block and a surface by measuring the force needed to move the block across the surfaces you supply. The children can use photocopiable page 75 to help plan their investigation and record their results.
- When they have finished, ask the children to draw a bar chart of the forces needed for different surfaces and to decide whether their results agree with their original ideas.

Differentiation
More able: Ask the children to suggest a way to make the surfaces even easier to slide over. Try out their ideas – were they correct?
Less able: Help the children find out which were the easiest and hardest surfaces for the blocks to slide over. *What differences can you see between these surfaces?*

Links to other topics
Personal safety/citizenship: Think about surfaces on which cyclists need to take special care, and why. Look at features (such as ridged soles) of footwear that make them safer on ice.

HOW MUCH?

Load your van

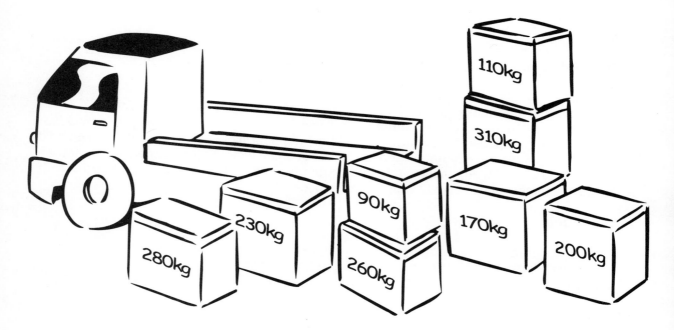

This van can carry a maximum of 600kg in a single load.

■ Investigate which of these crates the van could carry at one time. One example has been given for you.

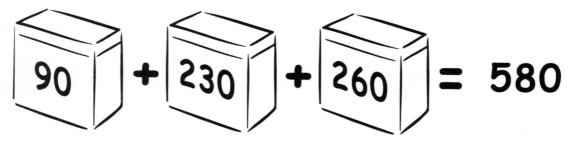

90 + 230 + 260 = 580

■ Make a general statement about how many crates the van can carry.

■ Give some examples that satisfy your statement.

NOW TRY THIS Find all the combinations of three crates that total exactly 600kg.

Load your van

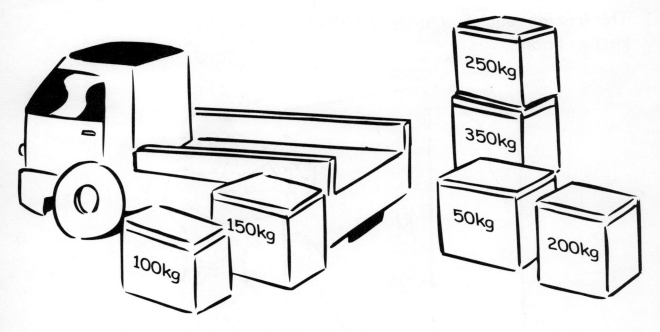

This van can carry a maximum of 600kg in a single load.

■ Investigate which of these crates the van could carry at one time. One example has been done for you.

$$100 + 150 + 250 = 500$$

■ What is the largest number of crates the van could carry? Give one example.

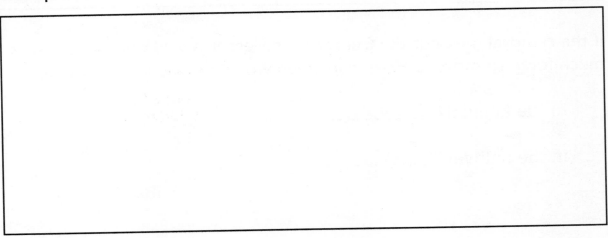

Moving house

This freezer requires a force of 350N to slide it across the kitchen floor.

One man can push the freezer with a force of 150N.
How many men will it take to move the freezer?

_____

In the hallway, it takes twice as much force to move the freezer.
How many men will be needed to push the freezer in the hallway?

_____

If the removal men put the freezer on rollers it would only need half as much force to move it. How many men would be needed to push it:

■ in the kitchen? _____

■ in the hallway? _____

What surfaces are easiest to slide on?

What question will you investigate?

Draw a labelled diagram to show what you do.

◼ Record your results.

What have you found out?

Is this what you expected?

SHINING BRIGHTLY

MATHS FOCUS: USING LANGUAGE RELATED TO MEASURES AND COMPARISONS

Learning objectives
- To use vocabulary related to measures.
- To suggest suitable units to estimate or measure mass or capacity.
- To suggest suitable measuring equipment.

Resources
- Three carrier bags, each similarly full of groceries. It's important that some bags contain heavy items and some contain light items.
- A range of apparatus for measuring capacity and weight, samples of different foods (such as flour, rice, dried peas, pasta, salt, cereals), containers of different volumes (spoons, yoghurt pots, different-sized lids, margarine tubs and so on), torches.
- Copies of photocopiable pages 78 (page 79 for less able children) and 80.

Introduction
5 mins
- Look at the carrier bags: *If you were helping carry the shopping, which bag would you carry? Why?* Expect argument here! *All the bags contain the same amount, they are all full.*
- Discuss what 'amount' can mean: 'how much room something takes up' (volume) or 'how heavy it is' (weight). Make sure the children are familiar with units for measuring both.

Whole-class, teacher-directed activity
10 mins
- Ask the children to suggest ways of comparing the 'amount' in each of the bags. Let them choose apparatus and units for measuring the volume or weight of each bag's contents. When they have decided, ask them to compare some of the carrier bags – now which would they choose?
- Show the children the food samples. *How can we compare these foods?* There are two ways: keep the volume constant and compare weights, or keep weight constant and compare volumes. Let the children look at the food samples to compare them.

Children's activity
20–25 mins
- Children should work in groups to compare foods, comparing either volumes or weights. They should use photocopiable page 78 to help them decide what apparatus to use, what to measure and how to make a fair comparison. Explain that they can use their own measures (such as 'which is easier to lift') if they can show that standard apparatus and measurements would be unsuitable.
- When they have finished investigating, ask the group to look at their results and to make a note of any conclusion they have reached.

Differentiation
More able: The children should use their results to work out the approximate weight of a carrier bag filled with one type of food. Make a note of any assumptions (such as the volume of the bag).
Less able: Help with planning by giving the children a specific task, such as: *Find out how much room 100g of each food takes up.* Use photocopiable page 79 to record results.

Plenary
10 mins
- Discuss how well the children's comparisons worked, thinking about accuracy and any limitations: 'The crisps should have taken up more room, but we squashed them.'

SCIENCE LINK ACTIVITY

Photocopiable page 80 gives children the opportunity to practise making comparisons in an unfamiliar situation. It asks the children to compare the brightness of two or three different torches, making decisions about how brightness can be described, measured and compared. The children can choose one of the suggested methods, or make up their own.

SHINING BRIGHTLY

SCIENCE FOCUS: CIRCUITS AND CONDUCTORS (QCA UNIT 4F)

Learning objectives
- To suggest ways to change the brightness of bulbs in a circuit.
- To make predictions about the effect of including additional batteries in a circuit.
- To plan to change one factor and keep others constant.

Resources
- Board or flip chart, marker pens.
- A selection of batteries, bulbs, wires (make sure that all the bulbs have the same voltage rating, and all batteries the same voltage; use reasonably new batteries to avoid the wide range of different voltages from a mixture of old and new batteries).
- Copies of photocopiable page 81.

Introduction
5–10 mins
- Draw a picture of a circuit on the board showing one bulb and one battery. Show the children how to build the circuit.
- Ask: *What would happen if we changed the number of batteries or bulbs?* If necessary, show the children how to add bulbs or batteries to the basic circuit.
- Explain that the children should predict, then test, how the brightness of the bulbs changes when the circuit changes. Ask: *How could you compare how bright the bulbs are?* (A direct comparison could note the distance at which light shows on a piece of white paper for each circuit.)

Whole-class, teacher-directed activity
15–20 mins
- Build a circuit comprising one bulb and one battery. Draw the circuit diagram on the board. Hide the batteries behind a board, but let the children see the bulb.
- Add another battery. Ask the children to look at the brightness of the bulb and suggest what has changed. Allow them to check, then ask a volunteer to change the diagram on the board to show the new circuit. Repeat with different numbers of batteries.
- Return to the basic circuit. This time, hide the bulb but show the batteries. Change the number of batteries. Ask children to predict how the brightness has changed based on the number of batteries they can see. Allow them to check.
- Ask the children what would happen if you had a circuit with one bulb, but kept on adding batteries. Demonstrate this (but try not to blow the bulb!). Show that the voltage written on bulbs and batteries tells us how many can be put together safely. Make sure you give children only a safe number of batteries to use and tell them not to use more in their circuits.

Children's activity
20–25 mins
- Ask the children to compare the brightness of bulbs in different circuits (one battery and one bulb, two batteries and one bulb, one battery and two bulbs and so on), using photocopiable page 81 to draw pictures of their circuits and record their results. Limiting the number of batteries available will ensure bulbs are not blown by putting too high a voltage across them.

Differentiation
More able: Replace a single bulb with two or three bulbs. Can the children predict the effect of changing the number of batteries now? Can they predict, then test, the changes in brightness when both the number of batteries and the number of bulbs are changed?
Less able: Help the children plan what to change (the number of bulbs) and what to keep the same (the number of batteries).

Links to other topics
Art: Look at pictures and paintings with light and shadow shadings. Ask the children to make a collage of scenes with lights of different brightness, such as festival scenes with candles (this could also link to a Diwali topic in RE), fairy lights, starlight and so on.

SHINING BRIGHTLY

Comparing different foods

◼ What do you want to find out? _____

_____

◼ What will you keep the same? _____

_____

◼ What will you measure? _____

_____

◼ Record your results. Remember to include the units you used.

Type of food	Weight	Volume

◼ Write down one thing you have found out from your experiment.

_____

_____

NOW TRY THIS Choose one type of food. How heavy would a carrier bag full of it be?

Comparing different foods

Our task is to find out _____

_____

We will keep the _____ the same each time.

Our results:

Type of food	What we measured

What did you find out?

We found out that _____

_____

_____

SHINING BRIGHTLY

Comparing torches

■ Describe how the light from torches is different.

How can you compare them? Here are some suggestions.
- What size area does the torch light up?
- What does it shine through?
- From how far away can you see it?

■ Draw a diagram to show what you will do. Label it.

What will you keep the same?

What will you measure?

Making bulbs brighter or dimmer

■ Look at this circuit.

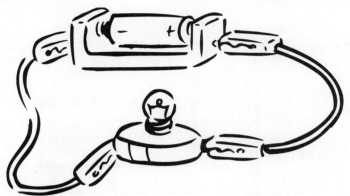

■ Name two things that could be changed.

■ Now change the number of bulbs in your circuit and see what happens. Draw the circuits you build.

What happened to the brightness?

■ Change the number of batteries. Draw your circuits and write what happened to the brightness.

■ Predict how bright the bulbs will be in a circuit with two batteries and two bulbs. Build the circuit to test your prediction.

MAKING ACCURATE MEASUREMENTS

MATHS FOCUS: READING MEASURING SCALES

Learning objectives
- To suggest suitable measuring equipment.
- To read measuring scales to the nearest division.

Resources
- A model measuring scale (see diagram), a range of measuring equipment (including thermometers, rulers and measuring cylinders/beakers).
- Scissors, glue.
- Copies of photocopiable pages 84 (page 85 for less able children) and 86.

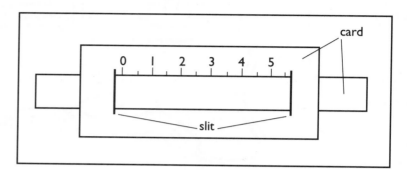

Introduction
5–10 mins
- Display the range of measuring equipment where everyone can see it. Look at some of the items that are used to measure and ask the children what they might measure with them (the width of a table, volume of water in a mug, temperature of tap water and so on).

Whole-class, teacher-directed activity
10 mins
- Ask: *What should we do if what we are measuring does not line up with one of the marks on the scale?* Show the children your model measuring scale clearly not lined up, and ask for suggestions how to read it. Help the children decide which division is nearest to the value being measured and read the scale to that division.
- Change the value on your model measuring scale. Read it again. Practise until the children are confident at reading the scale to the nearest division.

Children's activity
25–30 mins
- Photocopiable page 84 provides children with a range of scales to read. Ask them to complete each of the measurements, then to use real measuring equipment to find the measurement, to the nearest division, of the values suggested on the worksheet, filling in both the reading and the unit on the sheet.

Differentiation
More able: Where appropriate, encourage the children to read the measuring scales to the nearest half division. Can they suggest other appropriate things to measure with the apparatus they have used?
Less able: Use photocopiable page 85, and give the children only measuring equipment that is comparatively easy to use (rulers divided into centimetres or half centimetres instead of millimetres, for example).

SCIENCE LINK ACTIVITY

Photocopiable page 86 requires the children to colour in the scales on four thermometers to show particular readings, then cut these out and match them to pictures showing scenes that would be at approximately the temperatures shown by the thermometers.

Plenary
10 mins
- Ask the children to tell you what measuring apparatus they chose to measure the values given on the photocopiable sheets, and to explain why they made that choice.
- Encourage volunteers to set the model measuring scale to particular values, such as *just under 5*, and ask others to decide if they are correct.

MAKING ACCURATE MEASUREMENTS

SCIENCE FOCUS: KEEPING WARM (QCA UNIT 4C)

Learning objectives

■ To make careful measurements of temperature at regular time intervals.
■ To record results in a table.
■ To know that some materials are good thermal insulators.

Resources

■ A hot drink in a mug, a range of different insulating materials (such as a blanket, cotton wool, fleece and bubble wrap), beakers, hot (but not boiling) water, thermometers, stopwatches or clocks that clearly show minutes, board or flip chart, marker pens.
■ Copies of photocopiable page 87.
Safety: Hot water should be hand hot from the tap only. Check it is not hot enough to scald.

Introduction

5 mins

■ Show the children the hot drink and ask: *What could I do with this drink to keep it warm for as long as possible?* Guide the children to thinking about wrapping the drink in something.
■ Gather some suggestions, then show the children your selection of insulating materials. Ask: *Does it matter what I wrap it in?*

Whole-class, teacher-directed activity

10–15 mins

■ Help the children to plan an activity to compare different insulating materials. Discuss what to do (wrap the mug in the insulating material), what to use (water is easier than coffee and behaves in the same way) and what to record (how quickly the liquid cools down).
■ Ask: *How can we measure how quickly the water cools down?* Help the children realise that they will need to measure the temperature at regular time intervals to see how long it takes to reach a particular, cool, temperature (about 30°C is appropriate, as this is still sufficiently above room temperature that the water will reach it fairly quickly).
■ Discuss how to make the test fair: *What should be changed?* (Only the insulating material.) *What should be kept the same?* (Everything else: the size of beaker, volume and initial temperature of water, thickness of insulator, time interval between temperature readings and so on).

Children's activity

30 mins

■ Working in groups, ask the children to carry out the experiment, giving one material to each group, asking them to wrap a beaker of hot water in their insulating material and to take readings of temperature at regular time intervals (every two or five minutes is slow enough to be practical, but frequent enough to show clearly how the temperature changes).
■ The children should record their results in the table on photocopiable page 87, then work out the time taken for the temperature of their sample to fall below 30°C and enter this value in a class table on the board.
■ Use a plenary session to compare the groups' results. Look at the times for different materials entered in the class table and decide which material was the best insulator (the one which cooled the water most slowly). Relate this to the choice of materials for winter clothes, duvets, sleeping bags and so on.

Differentiation

More able: Children should take temperature readings every two minutes, not every five. Can they suggest what effect a thicker or thinner layer of insulating material would have on results?
Less able: These children may need help in co-ordinating both the stopwatch and thermometer readings. Aim to take readings only every five minutes, giving time to enter the reading in the table and prepare for the next reading.

Links to other topics

Science: Look at animal adaptations, such as thick fur coats for animals in cold climates.
History: Look at clothing from different times.

MAKING ACCURATE MEASUREMENTS

What does it read?

Look at these pieces of measuring apparatus. Write the reading next to each one. Remember to include the units.

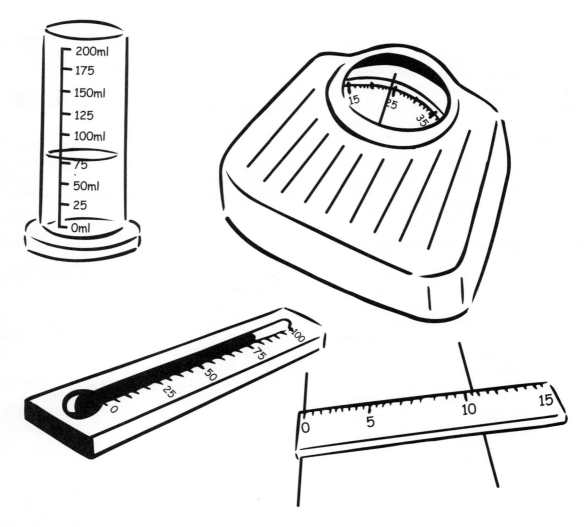

Now use suitable measuring apparatus to find these answers.

How much water does a mug hold? _____

How wide is this worksheet? _____

How heavy are you? _____

What temperature is the classroom? _____

NOW TRY THIS Can you read all the measurements above to the nearest half division?

MAKING ACCURATE MEASUREMENTS

What does it read?

■ Look at these pieces of measuring apparatus. Write the reading next to each one.

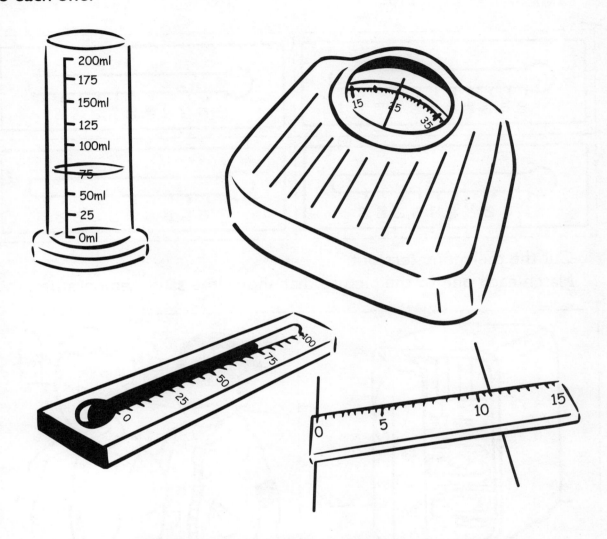

■ Use the measuring apparatus you have been given to find out:

  ▪ how heavy you are

I weigh _____ kg

  ▪ how warm the classroom is

The temperature is _____ °C

 NOW TRY THIS What other things could you measure with these pieces of apparatus?

MAKING ACCURATE MEASUREMENTS

How hot is it?

▨ Colour these thermometers so they show the temperatures below.

10°C   60°C   20°C   2°C

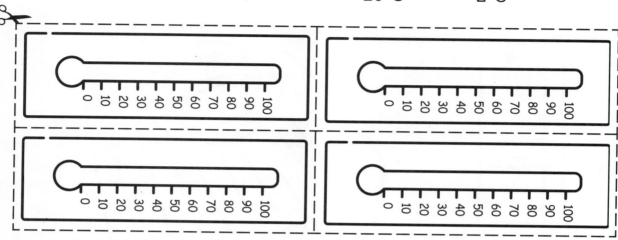

▨ Cut the thermometers out.
▨ Match each one to the picture that shows the same temperature.

MAKING ACCURATE MEASUREMENTS

Keeping drinks warm

■ Draw a picture to show what you did.

■ List three things you kept the same.

■ Record your results in this table

Time (minutes)	Temperature of water (°C)

■ Complete these sentences.

The insulating material we used was _____. It took

_____ minutes for our beaker of water to fall below 30°C.

■ Look at all of the results in your class. Which do you think was the best insulating material? Why?

TURNING AND BENDING

MATHS FOCUS: RECOGNISING ANGLES

Learning objectives
- To know that angles are measured in degrees.
- To estimate, draw and measure angles.
- To start to order a set of angles each less than 180°.

Resources
- 45° and 60° set squares, objects that use rotation (such as direction compasses, analogue clocks, pictures of control knobs from household appliances).
- A5 cards with angles of 30°, 45°, 60°, 90°, 120°, 135° and 180° drawn on them.
- Copies of photocopiable pages 90 (page 91 for less able children) and 92.

Introduction
10 mins
- Make sure the children understand the terms *full turn, half turn, quarter turn, clockwise* and *anticlockwise*. Look at some objects or pictures of objects that turn. Give quick-fire instructions such as: *Ben, stand up and make a half turn clockwise; Lisa, turn the clock hand a quarter turn anticlockwise.*
- Explain that angles are measured in degrees. A big angle has a big number of degrees.

Whole-class, teacher-directed activity
10–15 mins
- Explain that when something turns a full turn it has moved through 360°. Demonstrate by turning a pointer (such as the hands of a clock) through a full turn.
- Help the children work out how many degrees the pointer has moved through for a half turn, a quarter turn, and half a quarter turn.
- Show the children how to measure angles of 30°, 45°, 60° and 90° using 60° and 45° set squares. Use several examples drawn on the board, extending to real examples in the classroom to practise measuring angles.

Children's activity
25–30 mins
- Give the children a copy each of photocopiable page 90 to complete (using a set square if necessary).
- When they have completed the sheet, ask pairs of children to practise drawing and measuring angles using set squares. In turn, one child should secretly draw an angle using a set square; the other child should measure the angle, writing the answer next to the drawing.

Differentiation
More able: Ask pairs of children to invent a simple maze of their own, like the one on photocopiable page 90.

Less able: Use photocopiable page 91, which concentrates on full, half and quarter turns, both clockwise and anticlockwise.

SCIENCE LINK ACTIVITY

Photocopiable page 92 looks at angles on the human body. Children should draw views of a person rotated through quarter, half and full turns (they could work in pairs to model these turns). For the second part of the sheet, allow them to use set squares to identify and draw examples of parts of the human body moving through different-sized angles.

Plenary
10 mins
- Work through the two mazes from the photocopiable worksheets with the children. (The mouse eats the cheese and the monster eats the little girl.) Who got the answer right?
- Show the children the A5 cards with angles marked on them one at a time. Ask individuals to measure the angle, then arrange the angles in order of size, smallest to largest.

TURNING AND BENDING

SCIENCE FOCUS: MOVING AND GROWING (QCA UNIT 4A)

Learning objective
■ To know that humans, and some other animals, are supported by bony skeletons.

Resources
■ A model of a human skeleton, books with simple labelled diagrams showing some joints and bones.
■ Set squares.
■ Copies of photocopiable page 93.

Introduction
15–20 mins
■ Ask: *Where do you have bones? Can you feel your bones anywhere?* (Ribs, skull, shins, fingers.) Make sure the children know that they all have a bony skeleton. *What do you think we have bones for?* Talk about the role bones play in protecting fragile and important parts of our bodies (such as the skull protecting the brain, or the ribs protecting the lungs), and in supporting our bodies so that we can move around.

Whole-class, teacher-directed activity
■ Show the children the model of a human skeleton. *Look at the skeleton and think carefully about which bits of your body can move. What do you notice?* (Our bones are hard and stiff. Our bodies only move at the joints, where bones join together.)
■ Ask the children to locate (on both the skeleton and their own bodies) and name as many joints as possible. Include tiny ones (finger or toe joints), and those they may not think of as joints (neck and spine).
■ Demonstrate joints that move in many directions (for example, wrist and shoulder), and those that only move in one direction (elbow). Ask the children to hold their arms out straight and compare them, perhaps in terms of length or straightness (some 'straight' arms are straighter than others), and to compare how far they can bend their thumbs back (warn them not to try too hard!) Explain that, just as hair and eye colour vary, we vary in how far some of our joints can move.

Children's activity
20–25 mins
■ Working in pairs, ask the children to explore ways in which their different joints can move, using photocopiable page 93 to record what they find. They should identify joints that move in many directions, and those that only move in one direction. Encourage them to estimate the angles that different joints can move through, then to use a set square to check their estimates. Children do not need to know the names of any individual bones – *leg bone, finger joint* and so on are all that is needed, although some children may find books with the 'real' names interesting.

Differentiation
More able: Discuss and try to explain why limb joints such as the knee and elbow do not move beyond the 180°, out-straight position. (If they did, our legs – and arms when we crawled – could buckle and we would keep falling over.)
Less able: Identify joints that move through large and small angles. Decide whether particular joints move through more or less than a right angle.

Links to other topics
Literacy: Read and write movement poems, including some about creatures without skeletons.
PE/drama: Make use of the full movement of our bodies for expression.

Angles everywhere!

■ Draw where the pointer points when it turns.

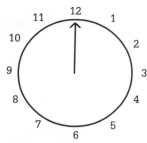

30° clockwise

60° anticlockwise

120° anticlockwise

150° clockwise

60° clockwise

30° anticlockwise

■ Follow the lines below. At each junction, the instructions tell you how far to turn the pointer. Use a protractor to help you.
■ Move along the path the pointer ends up pointing to.
Which treat will the mouse eat?

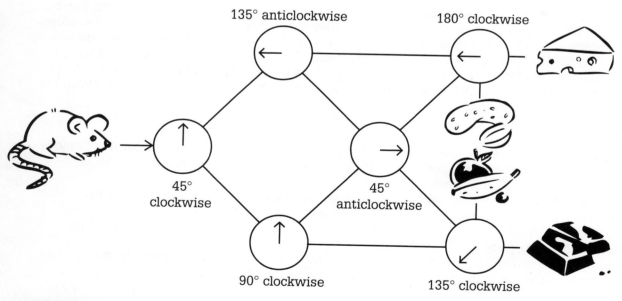

135° anticlockwise   180° clockwise

45°
clockwise

45°
anticlockwise

90° clockwise   135° clockwise

**NOW
TRY
THIS**   Can you make up your own mouse maze?

Turns and angles

■ Draw where the pointer points to when it turns:

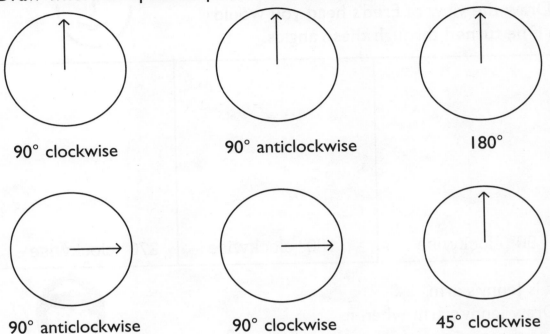

90° clockwise   90° anticlockwise   180°

90° anticlockwise   90° clockwise   45° clockwise

■ Follow the lines. At each junction, the instructions tell you how far to turn the pointer. Use a set square to help you.
■ Move along the path the pointer ends up pointing to.
Who will the monster eat?

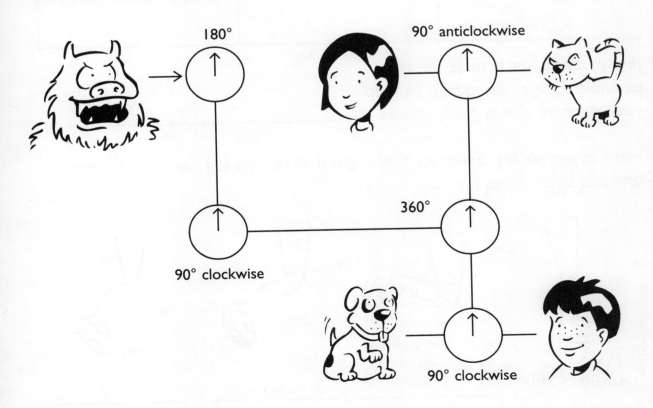

TURNING AND BENDING

Moving our bodies

This is Fred.

■ Draw the view of Fred's head you would see if he turned through these angles.

90° clockwise	180° clockwise	270° clockwise

This is Jenny's arm.

■ Draw Jenny's arm when it makes these angles.

45°	90°	135°

Jenny bends her arm as far as possible. Use a set square to help you estimate the angle it makes. _____

Here is Jenny's leg. Estimate the angle that Jenny's leg makes. The first one has been done for you.

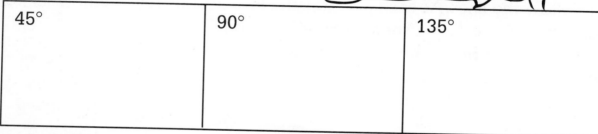

Angle = 180°   _____   _____   _____

TURNING AND BENDING

Exploring our joints

Some joints bend in only one direction, some bend in many ways.

■ Complete the table with as many different joints as you can find.

Joints that bend in one direction	Joints that bend in many directions

■ Some joints bend more than others. Choose six different joints and fill in the table.

Joint	How far we estimated it would bend	How far we measured it would bend

■ Why do you think knees and elbows only bend in one direction?

SORTING AND SEPARATING

MATHS FOCUS: SORTING WITH VENN DIAGRAMS

Learning objective
- To use a Venn diagram with two criteria to display information.

Resources
- Board or flip chart, marker pens.
- A variety of solids (such as marbles, cubes, sand, rice, peas, pasta), a colander (or a margarine tub with holes large enough to let some solids through).
- Copies of photocopiable pages 96 (page 97 for less able children), 98 and resource page 127.

Introduction
5 mins
- Write the number 20 on the board. Explain to the children that we can describe the number 20 in lots of ways: an even number, a multiple of 10 and so on. *Can you think of any more ways?* Repeat with other numbers.

Whole-class, teacher-directed activity
15 mins
- Look at Venn diagram 1 on an enlarged copy of resource page 127. Label the circle 'multiples of 5', then help the children decide where to place numbers you give them. Can they think of other numbers that would go inside or outside the circle?
- Repeat using Venn diagram 2 from the resource page, with the two circles labelled 'multiples of 5' and 'multiples of 2'. Ask the children to place numbers again, avoiding any multiples of both 5 and 2.
- When the children are confident with this, give them some numbers that can fit in both circles and introduce the idea of circles overlapping. Can the children think of examples to go in neither circle, each circle separately, and where both circles overlap?

Children's activity
25–30 mins
- The children should work individually to complete photocopiable page 96, first placing the numbers in the correct circles on the top Venn diagram, then using the characteristics of numbers in a completed Venn diagram to choose suitable labels for each circle.

Differentiation
More able: Ask the children to work in pairs to invent Venn diagrams for one another, or to work out the labels for a completed Venn diagram.
Less able: These children should work in pairs to complete photocopiable page 97.

Plenary
10 mins
- Look at the Venn diagrams on photocopiable page 96. Ask the children to volunteer some more numbers to fit in each section. Ask others to explain how they worked out the labels for the unlabelled Venn diagram. If appropriate, you could briefly introduce the idea of a Venn diagram with three circles. (Most children will not be ready to tackle this, but more able children may enjoy playing with the idea.)

SCIENCE LINK ACTIVITY

Show the children your collection of different solids and the sieve. Let the children experiment to find out which solids will pass through the sieve and which won't. Ask them to record their results in a 'one-circle' Venn diagram, then discuss other ways the solids could be grouped (for example, 'Edible'/ 'Not edible'). Ask the children to work in pairs on photocopiable page 98, making a Venn diagram to group the solids according to those that pass through the colander and those that can be eaten.

SORTING AND SEPARATING

SCIENCE FOCUS: SOLIDS, LIQUIDS AND HOW THEY CAN BE SEPARATED (QCA UNIT 4D)

Learning objectives
- To know that solids can be mixed, and that it is often possible to get the original materials back from a mixture.
- To choose appropriate apparatus for separating a mixture of solids.

Resources
- A variety of solids (such as marbles, cubes, sand, rice, peas, pasta).
- Three different mixtures of solids for each group – mixture 1: two solids of similar particle size, one with particles that roll, one without (such as marbles/cubes); mixture 2: two solids of very different particle size, neither of which roll (sand/pasta); mixture 3: two solids of very different particle size, one that will roll, one that won't (sand/dried peas).
- A sieve (or a margarine tub with holes), large bowl and flat tray for each group.
- Copies of photocopiable page 99 and resource page 127.

Safety: Do not use nuts in your mixtures of solids – some children may be allergic to them.

Introduction
5 mins
- Show the children your collection of solids. Discuss the different properties (size and shape) they have, and ask the children to suggest how they could use the properties of the solids to separate mixtures of two different solids.

Whole-class, teacher-directed activity
15 mins
- Pass two trays round the class: a tray of mixed marbles and cubes and a tray of sand and peas. Let the children try out the effect of tilting the trays or shaking them gently. Notice that the round objects roll down the slope while the others don't; and that when shaken gently, the smaller objects fall to the bottom of the tray.
- Show the children that some solids will pass through the holes in a sieve and others won't (the sieve method).
- Then show them that if a flat tray is tilted *slightly* and tapped *gently* (the tip-tap method), some solids will roll down the tray, and some won't.
- Demonstrate that shaking a mixture gently (the shake method) sometimes makes one solid 'settle out'. Discuss how each method might be used to separate different mixtures of solids.
- On resource page 127, help the children to decide how they would record mixtures that were separated in different ways. Discuss how they would show these in the Venn diagram, or how they could invent their own diagram to display their results.

Children's activity
20–25 mins
- Ask the children to work in small groups to explore how mixtures of different solids can be separated. Each group should find a way to separate the solids in each of mixtures 1, 2 and 3, then try to find ways of separating mixtures they have prepared themselves.
- Encourage the groups to try methods other than those discussed in the whole-class session if they wish. Photocopiable page 99 and resource page 127 can be used to record the mixtures used and the successful methods of separating them.

Differentiation
More able: Encourage the children to work with their own mixtures and methods. If appropriate, encourage them to try separating a mixture of three or more different solids.
Less able: Children may need support in deciding which method to use to separate given mixtures. Encourage them to try all methods and decide which works. They may need help in completing the Venn diagram – you might like to omit this part of photocopiable page 99.

Links to other topics
Art: Use different types/textures of dried materials to produce collages.

SORTING AND SEPARATING

Venn diagrams

◼ Put these numbers in the correct places on the Venn diagram.

12	5	28	40	45

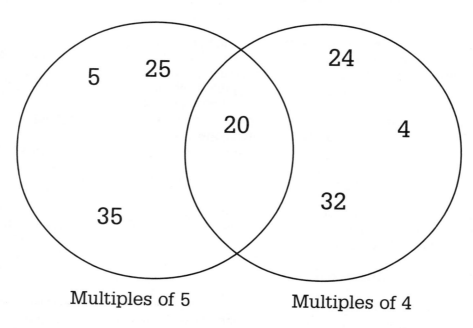

Multiples of 5   Multiples of 4

◼ Now write some more numbers in the circles on the Venn diagram.

◼ Look at this Venn diagram. Write labels for each circle.

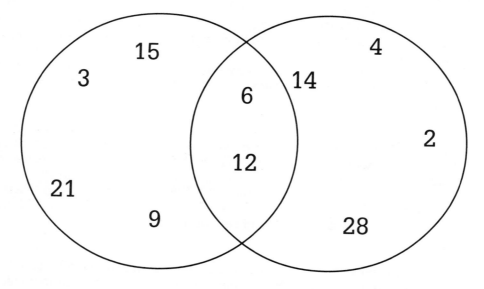

Can you invent some Venn diagrams of your own?

Venn diagrams

■ Put these numbers in the right places on the Venn diagram.

| 5 | 6 | 12 | 15 | 17 | 20 |

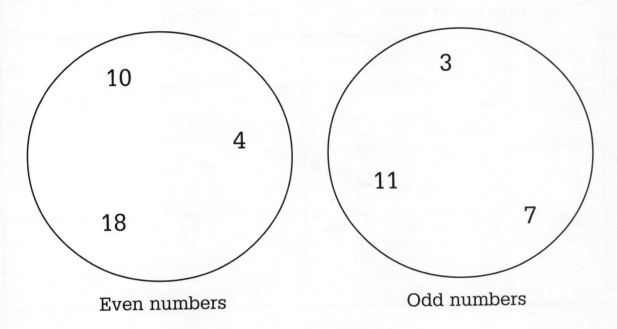

Even numbers   Odd numbers

■ Do you think the circles will ever overlap?

■ Look at this Venn diagram. Label the second circle.

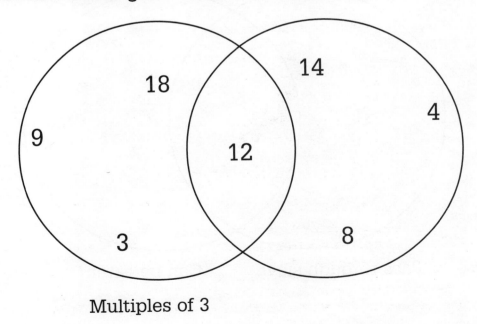

Multiples of 3

■ Add one more number to each circle of this Venn diagram.

SORTING AND SEPARATING

Grouping different solids

■ Group your solids in two lists. Some of your solids might be in both lists.

Pass through the sieve	Can be eaten

■ Show your results in a Venn diagram.

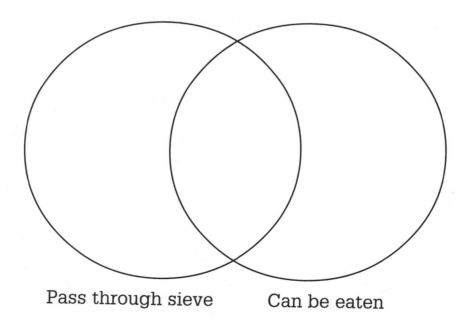

Pass through sieve   Can be eaten

NOW TRY THIS Can you think of any other ways to group your solids?

SORTING AND SEPARATING

Separating mixtures of solids

Here are three ways of separating mixtures of solids.

■ List some mixtures you separated using each method.

Sieving	Tip-tap method	Shaking

■ Show some of your results as a Venn diagram

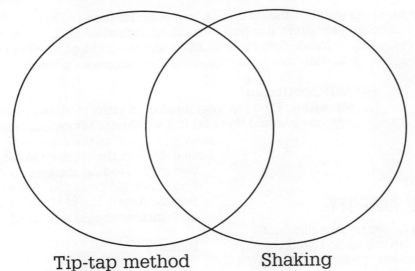

Tip-tap method   Shaking

NOW TRY THIS

Find a way to separate a mixture of three solids.
Explain what you did.

WILDLIFE INVESTIGATIONS

MATHS FOCUS: COLLECTING DATA TO SOLVE A PROBLEM

Learning objectives
- To collect data using a tally chart.
- To represent information on a pictogram where one picture represents several units.
- To understand language associated with data collection, representation and interpretation.

Resources
- Bird feeders (these can be bought from garden centres, but can be as simple as small, shallow trays) with four different types of food (such as peanuts, birdseed, bread, water).
- Each child will need: a clipboard and pencil, copies of photocopiable pages 102 (page 103 for less able children), 104 and resource page 125.
- Access to different types of habitat (playground, grass, plant tubs/stones/logs, under hedge).
- An A3 copy of resource page 125.

Preparation: Set up four bird 'stations' at least a week before the lesson (so the birds get used to them), each with a different food. Put each station in a similar location in terms of height, distance from trees and so on. More birds will visit in autumn or winter than spring or summer.

Safety: Children should wash their hands after handling insects or soil.

Introduction
5 mins
- Ask: *Who has seen the bird feeders outside? Does anyone know what they have in them? Has anyone seen any birds visiting them? How many birds are visiting our feeders? How could we find out?* Remind the children how to make tally charts.

Whole-class, teacher-directed activity
20 mins
- Give the children a clipboard each and a copy of photocopiable page 102. Ask them to spend 20 minutes (quietly!) recording in the tally chart the number of birds visiting the stations.
- Back in the classroom, explain that you want to make a pictogram of the results. Decide on a title and labels for the enlarged copy of resource page 125. Show that the pictogram will not fit on the page if one picture represents one bird. Ask for ideas, then show how using one picture for two or five birds makes the pictogram fit the page.

Children's activity
20–25 mins
- Working in groups, the children should decide on a scale for their pictogram, then draw a labelled pictogram showing how many birds visited each feeding station.
- When they have finished, ask the children to work out which station was most popular, and to suggest a possible reason.

Differentiation
More able: Find the total number of visits to all the feeding stations – how many would there be in a whole day? Does this represent the number of birds in the area?

Less able: Ask the children to tally visits to only two of the feeding stations, and use photocopiable page 103 to record their results. Advise the children how many birds each picture should represent.

Plenary
10 mins
Look at the children's pictograms: *Are they all the same?* (Probably not – bird visits are not easy to count, and groups will have used different scales.) How could accuracy be improved?

SCIENCE LINK ACTIVITY

Ask the children to choose four different habitats around the school and predict which will have most insects. They should tally the number of insects found in each habitat using a copy of photocopiable page 104, then make a pictogram using resource page 125. Was the prediction correct for your school? Would it be the same elsewhere?

WILDLIFE INVESTIGATIONS

SCIENCE FOCUS: HABITATS (QCA UNIT 4B)

Learning objectives
- To pose questions and make predictions about the habitats in which organisms live.
- To design a fair test and collect evidence.
- To make reliable observations and use these to draw conclusions.

Resources
- Pictures of insects (especially woodlice).
- Large shallow trays, sand, gravel, potting compost, water, jugs or beakers, stones or pebbles, bark chippings, leaves, woodlice (collect them just before the lesson, and release them immediately after).
- Copies of photocopiable page 105 and resource page 125.

Preparation: Placing several large pots, stones or logs on damp soil a few days before this activity will make woodlice much easier to find. Adjust the size of your groups or the number of woodlice for each group according to how many creatures you have been able to collect.

Safety: Do not collect materials from areas that may have been soiled by animal faeces. Insects can be collected safely using a 'pooter' (available from secondary schools) or using a scoop and soft paintbrush.

Introduction
10 mins
- Remind the children of their work on insects. Show them a picture of a woodlouse: *Can anyone remember finding insects like these? Where do you think they like to live?*
- Ask the children to think about the conditions that woodlice might like to live in. Help them to think of wet, damp, dry, dark, light, shady and so on. Encourage the children to suggest ways in which the preferences of woodlice could be tested.

Whole-class, teacher-directed activity
10–15 mins
- Tell the children that, in their groups, they are going to provide two or three different habitats (wet/damp/dry or dark/shady/light) in a tray to see which one woodlice prefer. Explain that each habitat has its advantages.
- Demonstrate how to make two or three different habitats in a shallow tray using your collection of natural materials (for example, areas of a tray covered by dry soil, damp soil and wet soil). Emphasise the need to make a clear dividing line between the different habitats and the need to place woodlice so that they can reach all habitats equally easily (fair testing).

Children's activity
20–25 mins
- Working in groups, ask the children to make their habitats in a shallow tray.
- When they are finished, the children should release 10 to 20 woodlice into their tray and leave them for about 30 minutes (until the woodlice seem to have stopped moving around).
- When the woodlice have settled, ask the goups to count the number of woodlice in each of their different habitats, recording their results on photocopiable page 105.
- The children should use their results to create a pictogram on resource page 125. Ask the groups to think about why investigating a large number of woodlice gives more reliable results than a small number.

Differentiation
More able: Ask the children to assess how reliable and realistic their results are: 'We used sand as a dry habitat, but perhaps the woodlice wouldn't have liked the sand even if it was damp.'
Less able: The children should concentrate on just two different types of habitat. Help them to decide how many woodlice each picture on their pictogram should represent.

Links to other topics
Citizenship: Link the activity with a visit to an environmental discovery centre looking at man's impact on different aspects of the environment. Your LEA or tourist board will be able to tell you about places in your area.

WILDLIFE INVESTIGATIONS

Bird table visitors

What is in your bird feeders? Record it in the tally chart below.

▢ Carry out a survey of the four feeding stations around the school, and keep a tally of how many birds visit each one over a five-minute period.

▢ Remember to keep quiet when you're watching so as not to disturb the birds!

Feeder	Tally	Total

▢ Fill in the 'Total' column of your tally chart.

▢ Now draw a pictogram on another sheet, showing the number of birds that visited each of your feeding stations.

▢ Decide how many birds are to represent by one picture on your pictogram.

Which feeder did most birds visit? _____

Suggest a reason why. _____

_____

_____

NOW TRY THIS What was the total number of bird visitors? How many bird visits would there be in a whole day?

WILDLIFE INVESTIGATIONS

Making a bird pictogram

What is in your two bird feeders?

_____   _____

■ Write these two foods in the 'Feeder' column of the tally chart.
■ Carry out a survey of your two feeding stations around the school, and keep a tally of how many birds visit each station in a ten-minute period. Remember to keep quiet when you're watching so that you don't disturb the birds!

Feeder	Tally	Total

■ Count your tally marks. Fill in the 'Total' column.
■ Now draw a pictogram of your results on another sheet.
■ Complete the following sentence:

One picture on the pictogram represents _____ birds.

Which feeder did most birds visit?_____

How many birds visited this feeder?_____

WILDLIFE INVESTIGATIONS

Finding minibeasts

Where might you find minibeasts around school? Predict four habitats around the school grounds where you might find them.

■ Write the names of the four places in your tally chart.

Predict which one will have most minibeasts. _____

Habitat	Tally	Total

■ On another sheet, make a pictogram to show the number of minibeasts in different habitats.

Which habitat had most minibeasts? _____

Was your prediction correct? _____

NOW TRY THIS Would your prediction be correct for a different school? Suggest a reason.

WILDLIFE INVESTIGATIONS

What habitats do woodlice like?

■ Draw your tray of habitats for woodlice. Label the different sections.

How long did you leave your woodlice for? _____

■ Record the number of woodlice in each habitat.

Habitat	Number of woodlice

■ Make a pictogram to show how many woodlice were in each habitat.
■ Write a sentence to describe what you have found out about the habitats woodlice like.

_____

_____

NOW TRY THIS How reliable do you think your results are?

HOW MANY, HOW MUCH?

MATHS FOCUS: DRAWING AND INTERPRETING BAR CHARTS

Learning objectives
- To use a bar chart to represent data.
- To interpret information from a bar chart to answer a question.

Resources
- Board or flip chart, marker pens.
- Copies of photocopiable pages 108 (page 109 for less able children), 110 and resource page 124 (one per child plus an enlarged copy).

Introduction
5 mins
- Tell the children that you want to draw a bar chart to show how many people are in the school hall at different times in the day. Discuss the basic features of a bar chart: *What will its title be? What will the labels on the axes be? What times will go along the x-axis?* ('clock' times, or 'assembly', 'before play' and so on are both acceptable.)
- Write the title, labels and times on your enlarged copy of resource page 124.

Whole-class, teacher-directed activity
15 mins
- Help the children write a 'diary' of a typical school day on the board, showing the times listed on your bar chart. Display the 'diary' where children can see it.
- Ask: *How many people are in the hall at...?* for each time in your diary. Colour in the same number of blocks in the first bar of your enlarged bar chart. Repeat for the other times.
- Now hide the diary. Use the completed bar chart to work out when there were most/least people in the hall. *How many children were there in the hall at the busiest time? Why?*

Children's activity
25–30 mins
- Give each child copies of photocopiable page 108 and resource page 124. Ask them to use the information on page 108 to plot a bar chart showing how many children walked to school each day during a two-week period.
- Once they have plotted their bar charts, the children should use the information for week 1 to suggest reasons why numbers were high and low, then use the bar chart to suggest what the weather was like on various days in week 2.

Differentiation
More able: Ask the children to show, in a different colour on their bar chart, what they think the numbers might be if the information was collected in summer instead of winter.

Less able: Give the children copies of photocopiable page 109 on which to base a bar chart for week 1 only, then ask them to relate the numbers on the bar chart to the information given about the weather and school events.

SCIENCE LINK ACTIVITY

The bar chart on photocopiable page 110 shows how the temperature of a drink taken on a picnic changes, together with a picture story showing what happens to the drink. The children have to relate the changes represented on the bar chart to the changes in the real world detailed in the story. They should decide when the temperature of the drink will be changing, how it will change, and find these points on the bar chart. (At 9:00am the drink is taken out of the fridge and begins to warm up; at 2:00pm it is returned to the fridge and begins to cool again.)

Plenary
10 mins
- Display an enlarged copy of the bar chart for week 1, (Do not show week two at this stage.) Discuss which days have the highest and lowest bars, and relate this to the circumstances the children thought about earlier.
- Now show the completed bar chart for week 2. Ask the children to suggest appropriate circumstances for these figures, justifying their choices.

HOW MANY, HOW MUCH?

SCIENCE FOCUS: KEEPING WARM (QCA UNIT 4C)

Learning objective
- To use ICT to collect, store and retrieve temperatures, and to explain trends and patterns in results in terms of scientific knowledge and understanding.

Resources
- Thermometers, mugs containing hot (but not boiling) drinks.
- A clock, a temperature sensor or data logger and computer software to present temperature sensor readings as a bar chart,
- Copies of photocopiable page 111.

Safety: Make sure the temperature of the drinks is not hot enough to scald. This activity will show a greater variation in temperature readings if done in winter rather than summer.

Introduction
5 mins
- Ask: *Can you think of some things that change temperature?* (Thermometers left clearly visible in hot drinks could be used to stimulate ideas.) Ask: *How quickly do you think the temperature of things changes?* Most children will probably be aware that some temperatures (such as that of a hot drink) will change quickly, while other temperatures (such as the temperature outside) change quite slowly.

Whole-class, teacher-directed activity
10–15 mins
- Show the children the temperature sensor. Explain that this can be used to measure the temperature in the classroom at regular time intervals.
- Demonstrate this on the computer by plotting a graph of the change in temperature as a mug of hot drink cools down. Encourage children to compare the temperature shown by the bar chart on the computer with that shown by an ordinary thermometer in the drink.

Children's activity
20–25 mins
- Ask the children to predict by how much and how quickly the temperature of the classroom will change over a period of 24 hours. When will it be hottest and coldest? Will some parts of the classroom be hotter than others?
- Place the temperature sensor in a position chosen by the children (by a radiator or on a windowsill in sunlight are good places; try to avoid shady corners) and leave it to take temperature readings over a span of 24 hours.
- When you have gathered the data, ask the children to work in small groups on copies of photocopiable page 111, using the computer to plot a bar chart of their results.
- Working in pairs, the children should use the bar chart to decide by how much the temperature is changing, and try to explain why these changes might occur (because it is night-time, the central heating gets switched on and so on).
- If possible, carry out this experiment in two or more positions around the classroom, asking children to compare the temperature changes in different places – can they suggest reasons for any differences in the two sets of results?

Differentiation
More able: Encourage the children to think of a range of things that might affect the temperature in the classroom. Ask them to predict the effect of particular changes, such as leaving the window open or the central heating breaking down.

Less able: Ask the children to identify, and highlight using coloured pencils, high and low temperatures on the bar chart. Help them, if appropriate, to identify areas of the bar chart where the temperature is getting higher or lower.

Links to other topics
ICT: Use ICT and a graphing program to plot bar charts and graphs. **Geography:** Look at the design of houses around the world (for example, houses in hot countries may have no glass in windows; in cold countries walls are insulated and windows are double- or triple-glazed.)

How many children walked to school?

This table shows the number of children in Class 4 who walked to school during the winter.

Date	Number who walked to school	Notes
Monday 7th	9	Cloudy
Tuesday 8th	4	Rainy
Wednesday 9th	1	Cycling proficiency test day
Thursday 10th	5	Icy
Friday 11th	14	Sunny
Monday 14th	12	
Tuesday 15th	12	
Wednesday 16th	9	
Thursday 17th	9	
Friday 18th	3	

■ Draw a bar chart showing the number of children who walked to school each day. (Ignore the days at the weekend.)
When did most children walk to school? Can you suggest why?

_____

_____

When did fewest children walk to school? Can you suggest why?

_____

_____

Look at the number of children who walked to school each day in the second week. What do you think the weather was like on each day? Write it in the table.

HOW MANY, HOW MUCH?

Walking to school

This table shows how many children from Class 4 walked to school one week.

Day	Number who walked to school	Notes
Monday	9	Cloudy
Tuesday	4	Rainy
Wednesday	1	Cycling proficiency test day
Thursday	5	
Friday	14	

■ Draw a bar chart to show the number of children who walked to school each day. Use your 'Bar chart' sheet.

How many children walked to school on Monday?_____

Why do you think only one child walked to school on Wednesday?

_____

■ Look at how many children walked to school on Thursday. What do you think the weather might have been like? Write it in the space in the table.
What do you think the weather was like on Friday? Write it in the table.

How does temperature change?

Mrs Smith went on a picnic.

This bar chart shows how the temperature of the can of drink changed over the day.

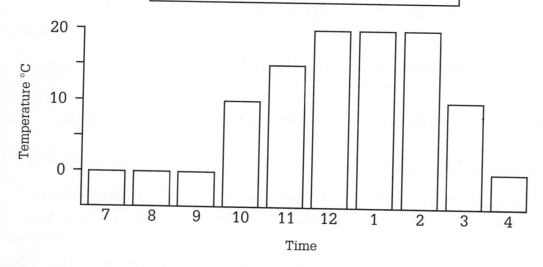

The temperature of Mrs Smith's drink

When did Mrs Smith take the can of drink out of the fridge?

_____

What was the temperature where Mrs Smith had her picnic?

_____

What was the temperature in the fridge?

_____

When did Mrs Smith put the can back in the fridge?

_____

HOW MANY, HOW MUCH?

When is it warmest?

■ In the space below, draw a plan of your classroom. Mark where you put the temperature sensor.

How long did you record the temperature for each time? _____

What was the highest temperature? When? _____

What was the lowest temperature? When? _____

What things might make the temperature change? Explain how the temperature in the classroom could change.

_____

_____

_____

Suggest something else that might also make the temperature change. What effect do you think it would have?

_____

_____

COMPARING BOYS AND GIRLS

MATHS FOCUS: USING BAR CHARTS TO MAKE COMPARISONS

Learning objectives
- To solve a problem by collecting and organising information.
- To present information as a bar chart.
- To use a bar chart to answer questions.

Resources
- Board or flip chart, marker pens.
- Copies of photocopiable pages 114–16.

Preparation: Each pair of children will need one copy of page 115 as it is, and one copy with height values along the x-axis: *less than 120cm, 120cm, 125cm, 130cm, 135cm, over 135cm.*

Introduction
5 mins
- Ask: *Do you think boys and girls can do the same things? Can boys run faster than girls? Can girls swim further than boys?* Allow children to suggest more ideas. Record some of their ideas on the board, then ask: *How could we find out if your ideas are correct?*

Whole-class, teacher-directed activity
15 mins
- Choose a class prediction about how boys and girls swim, such as: 'We think that girls can swim further than boys.' Write this on the board, and talk about what information would have to be collected to test this prediction.
- Draw two frequency tables on the board – one for boys and one for girls – showing how many children can swim each distance. If you use six different lengths (*less than 5 lengths, 5, 10, 15, 20 lengths, more than 20 lengths*), this will make it easy for the children to transfer the information to the bar charts on the blank copy of photocopiable page 115.
- Collect, by a show of hands, information about how many lengths the children can swim. Ask them to round the number of lengths they can swim to the nearest five lengths, helping them where necessary. Fill in the class frequency tables on the board.

Children's activity
25–30 mins
- Ask pairs of children to use the information from the class frequency tables, and a copy of photocopiable page 115, to plot bar charts showing how far boys and girls can swim.
  - They should record the original class prediction on photocopiable page 114, then use their bar charts to find the most common number of lengths each gender can swim and decide whether or not their original prediction was correct.

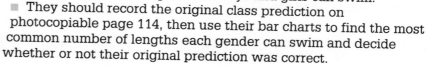

Differentiation
More able: Ask children to consider what would be the best number of children to look at for a reliable answer – a group? A class? The whole school? Why?

Less able: Give help when transferring information from the class frequency tables to the bar charts. Children may also need help interpreting the bar charts.

SCIENCE LINK ACTIVITY

Photocopiable page 116 asks the children to use information they are given to make a prediction, then plot bar charts showing the heights of a group of boys and girls (use the modified copy of photocopiable page 115 for this). They should then use their bar charts to draw a conclusion and decide whether or not this agrees with what they thought initially. It also asks them to discuss possible reasons for differences in the bar charts.

Plenary
10 mins
- Ask the class to help you write a summary of what they have found out on the board. Do they think they would get the same result comparing children in Year 4 with children in Year R, or a group of adults? Can they suggest reasons for their thoughts?

COMPARING BOYS AND GIRLS

SCIENCE FOCUS: MOVING AND GROWING (QCA UNIT 4A)

Learning objectives
- To know that human skeletons are internal and grow as humans grow.
- To identify a question and turn it into a form that can be tested, making a prediction.
- To decide what body measurement to make, and make it.
- To say what evidence shows and whether it supports a prediction.

Resources
- A chart or poster showing the development of a human from baby to adult.
- Tape measures.
- Copies of photocopiable pages 115 and 117.

Introduction
5 mins
- Show the children the poster detailing the development from baby to adult. Ask: *How does a human change as it grows up?* Encourage ideas about the change in proportion (especially the size of the head in relation to the body) as well as the change in size. *How do you think the baby's bones change? Do you think everyone in this class will have bones that are the same size?*

Whole-class, teacher-directed activity
10–15 mins
- Help the class express ideas about how the children's bones differ in a form that can be investigated as a class, for example: 'Who has the longest arms – boys or girls?', or 'Are the girls' heads bigger than the boys' heads?' (Expect giggles and argument here!)
- Ask for a class prediction, such as: 'We think boys have longer arms than girls.'
- Help the children to decide what information they would have to collect, and what measurements they would have to take to investigate their question.
- Discuss ways of making the results as accurate and reliable as possible: measurements should be recorded to the nearest centimetre, and should always be to the same point on each child; measurements should be repeated to improve reliability.
- Help the children decide how to record and present their results (tally charts and bar charts are best), reminding them if necessary of the methods they used in the maths activity. Recap on how bar charts can be used to make a comparison.

Children's activity
20–25 mins
- Working in groups, the children should decide on a question to investigate (ideally this should be different to the class question investigated above, but less confident children could repeat the class question), predicting what the answer will be. They should decide what measurements to take and how to make their results as accurate and reliable as possible (comparisons will be more valid if children take measurements for the whole class, so increasing the number of children in their survey).
- Ask the children to work together to make their measurements, record them in the tally charts on photocopiable page 117 and generate a frequency chart. The children should then draw bar charts using a copy of photocopiable page 115. When they have done this, ask them to use their charts to decide whether their results support their original prediction.

Differentiation
More able: Ask the children to suggest, and justify, how their results might differ if they looked at Year 6 children or at a group of adults.
Less able: Put the children into single-sex groups and ask them to collect information for either boys or girls. Provide adult help to compare their results with those of an opposite-sex group.

Links to other topics
Healthy eating: Look at how the correct balance of foods is needed to make bones grow strong and healthy. **History:** Look at pictures or samples of fossils and skeletons to compare historical animals with those around today.

COMPARING BOYS AND GIRLS

Comparing how far boys and girls swim

Can girls swim further than boys? Record your class prediction here.

_____

_____

■ Use the sheet 'Making bar charts' to plot a bar chart showing how far boys can swim.

■ Plot another bar chart showing how far girls can swim.

■ Look at the most popular values for each bar chart.

Who do you think can swim further, boys or girls? _____

Was your original class prediction correct? _____

Do you think the result would always be the same? _____

_____

NOW TRY THIS In this investigation, is it better to ask a large number or a small number of children how far they can swim? Why?

COMPARING BOYS AND GIRLS

Making bar charts

■ Complete the title.

Bar charts to show _____

Boys   Girls

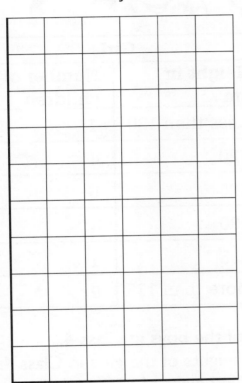   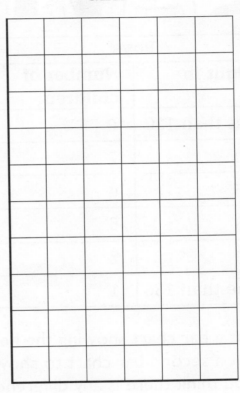

The most popular value is   The most popular value is

_____   _____

■ Our bar charts show that _____

_____

_____

_____

COMPARING BOYS AND GIRLS

Comparing heights of boys and girls

■ These frequency tables show how tall the boys and girls in Class 4 are.

Boys			Girls	
Height in cm	**Number of children**		**Height in cm**	**Number of children**
Less than 120	0		Less than 120	1
120	2		120	4
125	4		125	5
130	6		130	4
135	2		135	1
More than 135	1		More than 135	0

■ Plot a bar chart showing the heights of the boys in Class 4.
■ Plot a second bar chart to show the heights of the girls in Class 4.
Do you think there is any difference in the height of boys and girls in Class 4?

_____

Do you think you would get the same result for boys and girls in your class?

_____

Can you suggest a reason for these results? _____

_____

_____

_____

COMPARING BOYS AND GIRLS

Bone investigation

What question about bones will you investigate? _____

_____

Predict what you will find out. _____

_____

■ What will you measure? _____

_____

Use the tally charts to record your results.

Boys		

Girls		

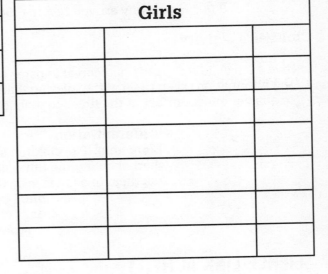

■ Plot separate bar charts for boys and girls.

Was your prediction correct?_____

NOW TRY THIS Would the results be the same if you looked at Year 6 children or adults?

UNDERSTANDING BAR CHARTS

MATHS FOCUS: INTERPRETING BAR CHARTS

Learning objective
▪ To solve a problem by representing and interpreting data in a bar chart.

Resources
▪ Board or flip chart, marker pens, A3 paper.
▪ Copies of photocopiable pages 120 (121 for less able children), 122 and resource page 124 (including an enlarged copy).

Preparation: On the day of this activity, ask all of the children to 'sign in' as soon as they arrive at school. Put an A3 sheet of paper up (on an appropriate door if children are not normally allowed in before school) 15 minutes before school starts and label it with the time. Change the paper for another labelled sheet 10 minutes before school starts, and repeat 5 minutes before school, when school starts, and 5 and 10 minutes after, remembering to ask the children to sign in as soon as they arrive. Keep the sheets for use in the lesson.

Introduction
5 mins
▪ Tell the children that this activity is about drawing and understanding bar charts. Ask: *Where have you met bar charts before?* Do they remember drawing bar charts in any of their maths or science activities? *Who thinks they could tell me how to draw a bar chart to show what time you all arrived at school today?*

Whole-class, teacher-directed activity
20 mins
▪ Ask: *What information would we need to collect to make a bar chart showing the times you all came to school today?* (The times and how many children arrived at each time.)
▪ Show the children the sheets they signed in on. Ask: *What times do we need to put along the x-axis?* Help the children work out some scales for the axes of a bar chart. Plot the information from the sheets on an enlarged copy of resource page 124.
▪ Help the children to answer questions about the bar chart, such as: *How many children arrived at 9:00? How many arrived before 8:50? When did most children arrive?*

Children's activity
20–25 mins
▪ Give each child a copy of photocopiable page 120. Ask them to complete it individually, using the information given to fill in the missing 'bars' on the bar chart, then interpret the bar chart to answer questions about the times that children arrived at school.

Differentiation
More able: The children should work in groups to decide what the bar chart showing the times children go home from school might look like. Ask them to explain why they have drawn it as they have.

Less able: Use photocopiable page 121. This sheet also asks children to think about the best scale to represent the information on the vertical axis.

SCIENCE LINK ACTIVITY

Photocopiable page 122 gives children practice at drawing and interpreting a bar chart showing how the time taken for different paper 'helicopters' to fall to the ground changes according to the length of the 'helicopter' wing.

Plenary
10 mins
▪ Ask a volunteer to describe how they made their bar chart showing school departure times. Focus on adding a title and labelling the axes. Ask other children to help where necessary. Ask less able children to explain how they can show information in a different way on bar charts with different axes.

SCIENCE FOCUS: FRICTION (QCA UNIT 4E)

Learning objectives
■ To plan a fair test, deciding what to change, what to keep the same and what to measure.
■ To identify a pattern in results and explain it in terms of air resistance and forces.

Resources
■ Graph or squared paper, scissors, string, paper clips.
■ Copies of photocopiable page 123 and resource page 124.
Safety: Consult your school safety guidelines before carrying out this activity because, in order to get successful results, children will need to stand on chairs to drop their parachutes or, for even better results, drop them down a stairwell. This activity will need to be supervised.

Introduction
5 mins
■ Ask: *Who can tell me something about parachutes?* Children may have seen parachutes being used in films or on television. They may be able to say what shape they are, what they are made from, and what they look like in the air or on the ground. *How long do parachutes take to come down?* At this level, children will know that some objects and materials are more 'floaty' than others; they may be able to identify things that will fall slowly, such as feathers and paper.

Whole-class, teacher-directed activity.
10–15 mins
■ Ask the children to suggest ways to investigate things that affect the time it takes a paper parachute to fall. *What might affect it? Could we investigate that?* Things that could be changed include: the height of drop (but this is impractical to test as a sufficient range of heights is difficult to obtain), area of parachute canopy, weight on parachute.
■ Discuss how to investigate the effect of changing the area of the parachute or the weight attached to it. Make sure the children understand the importance of changing only one thing at once. List what needs to be kept the same for each investigation and what needs to be measured – children can time the fall most easily by counting quickly from the point of drop and recording the number they reach when the parachute hits the floor.

Children's activity
20–25 mins
■ Working in small groups, the children should investigate the effect of changing *either* the area of the parachute *or* the weight on the parachute – you could either allocate an investigation to each group or allow them to choose.
■ Photocopiable page 123 can be used to guide the investigation and recording of results. The children investigating area should fold the paper, not cut it, in order to keep the weight the same. Resource page 124 can be used to plot a bar chart of the children's results.
■ Use a plenary session to establish that large parachutes fall more slowly because there is more air resistance slowing the parachute down, and heavy parachutes fall more quickly because the force pulling them down (weight due to gravity) is bigger.

Differentiation
More able: Ask the children to write a conclusion to explain what they have found out. Can they suggest ways to improve the reliability of their results from this activity?
Less able: The children may need support with deciding how to make the investigation fair (changing only one thing – area *or* weight – and keeping everything else the same, counting at the same speed each time, dropping the parachute from the same height). Decide what type of parachute would be best in real life.

Links to other topics
Design and technology/history: Look at and make models of other types of non-powered aircraft, such as hot-air balloons and gliders.

UNDERSTANDING BAR CHARTS

Time of arrival

Jubilee Primary School has 300 pupils.
School starts at 9:00am. The bar chart shows
the time children arrive in the morning.

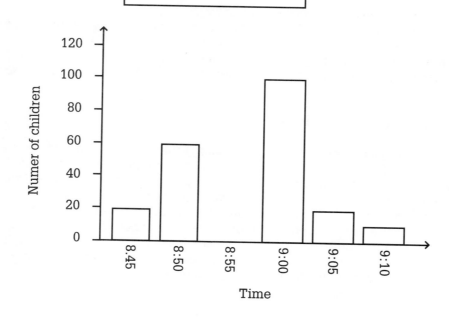

■ 80 children arrived at 8:55am. Show this on the bar chart.

■ Answer these questions:

How many children arrived at 8:50am? _____

How many children were away? _____

How many children arrived at school late? _____

NOW TRY THIS School ends at 3:20pm. On the 'Bar chart' sheet, draw a bar chart to show the times children go home. Why have you drawn it like this?

UNDERSTANDING BAR CHARTS

What time did they arrive?

There are 45 pupils in Year 4 at Jubilee Primary School. School starts at 9:00am. The bar chart shows when children in Year 4 arrive in the morning.

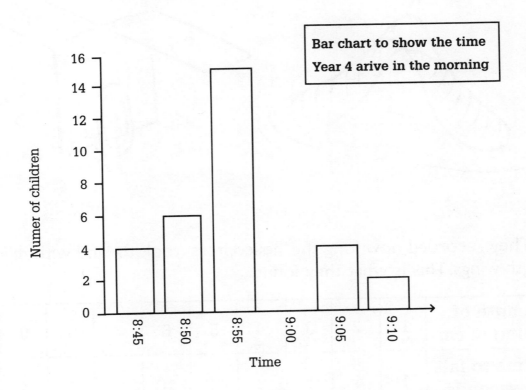

Bar chart to show the time
Year 4 arive in the morning

■ 12 children arrived at 9:00am. Draw this on the bar chart.

■ Answer these questions:

How many children arrived at 8:55am?_____

How many children were away?_____

How many children arrived at school late?_____

NOW TRY THIS

Kieran said, "It would be better if we labelled each square on the y-axis as five children, not two." Why is he wrong?

UNDERSTANDING BAR CHARTS

Making the best helicopter

The children in Class 4 watched tree seeds falling and decided to make their own model 'helicopters' to see which floated down best.

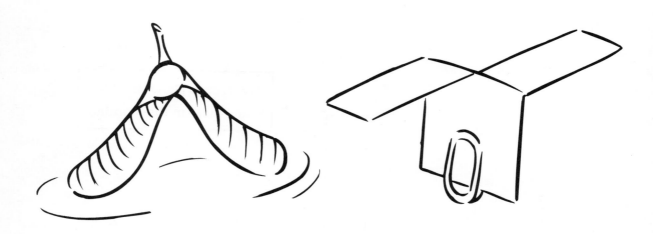

■ They recorded how long the 'helicopters' took to land with different length wings. This is what they found.

Length of wing in cm	1	2	3	4	5	6	7	8	9	10
Time to fall in seconds	1	4	7	8	10	10	9	6	4	2

■ On the 'Bar chart' sheet, plot a bar chart to show Class 4's results.

What is the best length wing for the helicopter? _____

Why? _____

_____

_____

_____

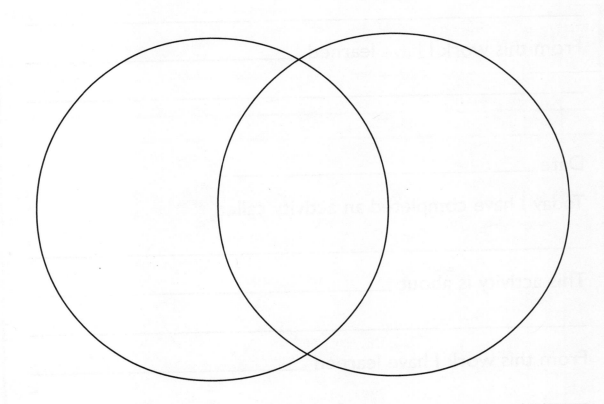

Name _____   Date _____

Date _____

Today I have completed an activity called

_____

This activity is about _____

_____

From this work I have learned _____

_____

Date _____

Today I have completed an activity called

_____

This activity is about _____

_____

From this work I have learned _____

_____

Date _____

Today I have completed an activity called

_____

This activity is about _____

_____

From this work I have learned _____

_____